THE CASE
THAT FOILED
FABIAN

THE CASE THAT FOILED FABIAN

MURDER AND WITCHCRAFT IN RURAL ENGLAND

SIMON READ

The History Press

To Cameron.
Love, Dad.

It is an old maxim of mine that when you have excluded the impossible, whatever remains, however improbable, must be the truth.

Sherlock Holmes in *The Adventure of the Beryl Coronet*.

First published 2014

The History Press
The Mill, Brimscombe Port
Stroud, Gloucestershire, GL5 2QG
www.thehistorypress.co.uk

© Simon Read, 2014

British Library Cataloguing in Publication Data.
A catalogue record for this book is available from the British
Library.

ISBN 978 0 7524 9357 2

Typesetting and origination by The History Press
Printed in Great Britain

CONTENTS

ACKNOWLEDGEMENTS

Although I live in California, I'm always looking for reasons to get back to Britain. Writing this book provided such an opportunity. Working on this project was a pure joy. The subject matter was intriguing, and it allowed me to spend some time in the Cotswolds. I never tire of the English countryside, so any chance to enjoy it is always welcome. No one ever writes a book alone – and this title is no exception. An author always relies on a support network of friends and family. In this case, I would like to start by thanking the good people at The History Press – especially Mark Beynon, my editor. This is the second book we've done together. We both share an enthusiasm for beer, scotch, classic British rock and James Bond. His excellent tastes aside, he's a great colleague and one I'm proud to call a friend. I owe my agents – Roger Williams in the States and Rachel Calder in the UK – a debt of gratitude for their tireless work on my behalf.

On the research front, I want to thank the staff at the National Archives in Kew. I've relied on them a good number of times, and they've never let me down. A very special thanks goes to Dick Kirby, crime author and retired Scotland Yard detective who spent eight years on the famed Flying Squad, for his assistance and pointing me in the right direction when I needed help. This book briefly examines Charles Walton's family history. I want to thank Richard Patterson – who has spent many years studying the Walton case – for providing me the findings of his genealogical research.

When, at the age of 13, I told my parents I wanted to be an author, they didn't dismiss the idea or try to talk me out of it – they encouraged me to pursue my ambition. I am incredibly grateful for their love, support, and friendship. Katie, my wife, read a first draft of this book and made great suggestions to help better the narrative flow. She's an amazing writer, and I hope to read one of her books someday. To my sons, Spencer and Cameron: I love you guys.

1

ORIGINS OF A MYSTERY

Charles Walton woke, as he always did, before sunrise and gingerly swung his legs out of bed. He placed his feet on the floor and slowly pushed himself off the mattress. Whether he went to work today or not was dependent on how badly his body ached. The 74-year-old suffered from rheumatism and sciatica. Standing, he grabbed his short walking stick and moved to the bedroom window. Only recently arthritis had started to bend the old man's body, forcing him to use the stick when he walked.

He lived in number 15, Lower Quinton, a thatched-roof cottage opposite the village church. Outside, the steeple stood in silhouette against the pre-dawn sky. Walton shared the cottage with his 33-year-old niece, Edith Walton. He and his wife had adopted her when she was just 3, following the death of her mother. When Walton's wife died in 1927, Edith became Walton's housekeeper. For her services, Walton paid his niece £1 a week. She didn't mind taking care of her uncle, for 'he was an extremely good-tempered man'. Not prone to anger, he never gossiped about others in the village and got along well with those he met in passing – but, the truth was, he preferred to keep to himself. 'He was friendly with everyone,' Edith would later recall, 'but no one ever visited him at the house. He didn't go out in the evenings and very seldom went into the public house. He was always happy and contented with his life.' Indeed, Walton's was a simple existence. He worked as a farm labourer and, for the past year, had worked trimming hedges for Alfred John Potter, owner of

The Firs Farm in Lower Quinton. The job, along with his old-age pension of 10s a week, allowed him to pay rent on the cottage and purchase 'coal and meat'.

Rare was the occasion Walton would work a full week. During the winter, he worked the odd day here and there, as the cold weather wreaked havoc with his arthritic bones. He was a man of ritual. On the days he did decide to work, he would leave the house at 8.30 a.m. and take with him only a piece of cake, which he ate for a midday snack. He never carried his hedging tools with him. Instead, he would leave them in whatever field he was working in at the time and simply resume where he left off in the morning. At 4 p.m., he would return home for dinner. The morning of Wednesday 14 February 1945 was like any other. Edith was in the kitchen when her uncle came downstairs, ready to start his day's labour. He wore a tweed jacket, a matching waistcoat and heather-mixture cardigan. To further protect him against the elements, he wrapped his wiry frame in a flannel body belt and two shirts – one made of flannel, the other short-sleeved and made of cotton. A pair of black boots and knitted socks kept his feet warm. It was the same outfit he wore whenever he went out hedging. Attached to a chain fastened to his waistcoat was a white metal pocket watch he carried with him at all times.

Walton never carried a wallet or personal papers. According to Edith, 'He sometimes carried a purse with a few shillings in it, but on the morning of 14th February 1945, he left it at home.' Edith, too, was preparing for work that morning. She had found employment as a typesetter at the Royal Society of Arts, which had vacated bomb-ravaged London for the safety of Lower Quinton. Charles took a seat at the small kitchen table as Edith prepared for him two pieces of toast and a cup of coffee – the same thing he ate every morning for breakfast. As Charles finished his meal, Edith wrapped a piece of cake for him in a blue sugar bag. The morning ritual complete, Charles left the cottage for the fields beneath Meon Hill. For the past several days, he had been trimming hedges in a field called Hillground.

The fact Walton met his end in the shadow of Meon Hill lends this mystery an air of the supernatural. The hill, home to foxes, rabbits, and badgers, rises 637 feet above the surrounding countryside. Despite the cultivation of Meon Hill by farmers over the centuries, the remnants of a fort dating back to the Iron Age are still visible as earthworks on top of the hill. Supposedly the inspiration for Weathertop in Tolkien's *The Lord of the Rings*, Meon Hill is the furthest of the Cotswold mounds and has long been the setting of strange and ghostly stories. Local legend suggests it was once the earthly domain of the Devil. In the eighth century, so one story goes, the Devil looked down from Meon Hill across the fields to the rising spire of the recently constructed Evesham Abbey. So enraged was the Devil by the Holy spectacle he kicked a massive boulder down the hill in an attempt to smash the edifice. His effort was thwarted, however, by local villagers who diverted the course of the boulder through the power of prayer. The rock, missing the Abbey completely, instead came to rest on Cleeve Hill, near Cheltenham, where villagers shaped it into a giant cross to keep the Devil away. A variation of the same story claims the Devil clawed a large clump of earth from a field and threw it at the Abbey. Again, the power of prayer did him in when the Bishop of Worcester beseeched God to send the massive projectile astray. The earth fell from the sky mid-flight and thus formed Meon Hill upon its landing. Another legend holds that the phantom hounds of an ancient Celtic king roam the hill's slopes at night. Supposedly, the 'king was the lord of departed spirits who would hunt to gather souls, riding a pale horse and accompanied by a pack of white hounds with red ears'.

Having finished breakfast, Walton bid his niece farewell for the day and left the cottage. He moved with the aid of two walking sticks – one he purchased, the other he had made from a rough branch cut from a hedge. From his home, he hobbled across the road and made his way through the churchyard opposite. The morning was grey and damp, the tombstones in the churchyard glistening with moisture in the cold early light. Edith watched him from the cottage doorway before she finished readying herself for the day. Returning from work at 6 p.m., there was no response when she walked through the door. She called her uncle's name and searched the cottage, and was surprised to discover the house empty. It was not like Walton to be out this late. She knew there was no point checking at the College Arms pub around the corner, for he wouldn't be there.

Bundling herself in a coat, she went back out and knocked on the door of Harry Beasley, who lived in the cottage directly next door. Beasley had known Walton all his life and had lived next door to him for twenty-three years. He had last seen Walton at 5 p.m. the previous day. Walton had been working in his garden and called over to Beasley for help putting a piece of wood on a sawhorse. The old man, Beasley later recalled, had been 'pleasant and friendly, just as usual'. When Beasley answered Edith's knock, he could tell by the expression on her face something was wrong.

'Uncle hasn't come home yet,' she said. 'Would you mind coming to see if we could find him?'

Beasley knew it was odd for Walton to be out after dark. For the past year, Walton had been 'bent nearly double with rheumatism' and had trouble getting around without his walking sticks. Beasley immediately agreed to help Edith with her search. He grabbed a coat and a torch and led Edith across the road. They passed through the churchyard, as Walton had done that morning, and entered the fields belonging to Alfred Potter. They wandered about aimlessly, calling out Walton's name, searching ditches and scanning fields, all to no avail. Each passing minute only served to stoke Edith's growing concern. She knew something had happened to her uncle. When it became apparent their search was going nowhere, they walked to Firs Farm to ask Potter for help. It was roughly 6.15 p.m. when Potter got up from the dinner table to answer the knock on his door.

'What hedge was my uncle working on?' Edith asked, foregoing any customary pleasantries. 'He has not returned home. There must be something wrong.'

'My God,' Potter replied, 'there must be.'

He led Edith and Beasley across the farmyard and back into the fields.

'I have to do the milking on Wednesday,' Potter explained, as they made their way in the dark. 'I came to the field to cut some hay at twelve o'clock and saw your uncle was at his work.'

Potter followed the path he assumed Walton would take on his way to and from work. Beasley walked alongside Potter, the light from their torches cutting a swathe through the misty black. Edith followed a few yards behind. The night swirled about them as a cold breeze blew off the slopes of Meon Hill, stirring the hedgerows and whispering through dead branches. They passed through a gate and into the field Potter had last seen Walton working that afternoon.

'This is the hedge he was on,' Potter said.

They followed the length of hedge Walton had been trimming. In a corner where the hedge intersected another, about 10 yards from where Potter had last seen Walton alive, they made the horrible discovery. Walton lay on the ground, his face glistening with blood. The two men stopped in their tracks. Immediately, Edith – still trailing behind them – knew something terrible had happened.

'I hadn't better let her see it,' Beasley said, his voice thick in his throat.

He turned to stop Edith from coming any closer – but it was too late, she was already screaming. Just at that moment, local farm labourer Harry Peachey passed on the other side of the hedgerow, walking in the direction of neighbouring Upper Quinton. Peachey worked for a local farmer and had gone up the hill to inspect a field of beans he had planted several months prior. On his way up, he had noticed nothing unusual. Now, on his way back down, it was obvious some sort of drama was unfolding in Potter's field.

'Peachey,' Potter shouted. 'Go down to Mr Valender's and phone the police to come up here at once!'

Peachey, hearing Edith's screams but unsure as to what, exactly, was happening, did as instructed. Potter watched him disappear into the darkness before turning his attention once more to the horror at his feet. A hayfork had been thrust through the old man's face; the handle had been pressed backwards and wedged under the hedge. The blade of Walton's trouncing hook was buried deep in his neck. Behind Potter, Beasley gently coaxed Edith away from the scene, leading her back through the fields and towards the village. Near the churchyard they encountered Potter's wife, Lilian.

Once Potter had gone off in search of Walton, Lilian had set about locking up the fowls for the evening. From the back of the farmhouse, she could see her husband – along with Harry Beasley and Edith – make their way through the orchard alongside the churchyard in the direction of the fields. As Lilian went about her evening chores, a neighbour, Miss Savory, stopped by and asked if she needed help. Glad for the company and the assistance, Lilian accepted. As the two women caged the hens for the night, Lilian mentioned 'the hedge cutter hadn't come home'. The news intrigued Miss Savory, who suggested the two of them go and investigate. The hens caged for the night, the two women left the farmyard in search of Potter and the others. They hadn't got far when they heard what sounded like someone shouting in surprise.

'That sounds like Alf's voice,' Lilian said.

It was not long thereafter they met on their way up Beasley, who accompanied the sobbing Edith.

'He's dead,' Beasley said, matter-of-factly.

'Where's Alf?' asked Lilian.

'He's got to stay there until I get back,' Beasley said, motioning over his shoulder.

The four of them walked back towards the village, Edith's wrenching sobs carrying across the darkened fields.

✻

Allan Raymond Valender owned a farm and bakery in Upper Quinton. Just that morning, shortly before noon, Edith had come to visit him in the bakehouse to enquire about a wireless radio he was selling. The two discussed the price, and she agreed to buy it for £7. Now, it was 6.45 p.m. He had just settled into an armchair in his sitting room when a loud rapping at the window made him jump. He put down his paper and went to the front door to investigate, surprised to find Peachey standing out front and struggling to catch his breath.

'I want you to phone the police immediately,' Peachey rasped. 'Mr Potter asked me to come down to you.'

'Why,' said Valender, 'what's wrong?'

'I don't know,' said Peachey, pausing, 'but I think there's something wrong with a girl. I think it's Edie Walton. It's just over in Mr Potter's field.'

Knowing Potter was not a man easily startled, Valender went back inside and telephoned the Warwickshire County Constabulary, located in the nearby village of Long Marston. Michael Lomasney, Police Constable 173, took the call. The time was 6.50 p.m.

'This is Ray Valender, Jim,' said the urgent voice on the end of the line. 'I've been told by Harry Peachey that there is a girl at the foot of Meon Hill and that there is something seriously wrong with her. I've been asked by Alf Potter to send for the police.'

'All right, Ray,' said Lomasney. 'I'll come at once.'

'You had better come to me at my place,' said Valender, 'and I'll come along with you.'

Lomasney donned his hat and grabbed the keys to the police car. He arrived at Valender's house at five minutes past the hour and saw Valender and Peachey waiting for him. The three men walked into the fields neighbouring Valender's house. They crossed two pastures and stopped.

'Where are you, Alf?' Valender shouted.

'Here I am,' called Potter, whose field adjoined Valender's land.

Lomasney moved in the direction of the voice and climbed a boundary fence into Potter's field. Potter stood about 25 feet from the corner of the field, near a Royal Air Force cable pole.

'Where is she, Alf?' asked Lomasney, concerned for the girl.

'Look over there in the corner,' Potter replied, pointing his finger in the direction where two hedges intersected.

Lomasney walked to the corner of the field and saw 'a man lying on his back with his head towards the hedge'. The last pale vestiges of the winter sun were long gone. In the darkness, the constable initially thought the corpse was that of a serviceman.

'It's an airman,' he said to no one in particular.

Potter mumbled something under his breath in response, but Lomasney was too focussed on the atrocity in front of him to hear what the farmer said. He pulled his lamp from his belt, threw some light on the dead man's face, and saw the victim was a civilian.

'Who is it, Alf?'

'It's old Charlie Walton,' Potter replied. 'He had been working for me at trimming the hedge.'

After having 'a good look at the body', Lomasney initially thought the death to be a case of suicide, though he did not indicate why in his eventual statement to Scotland Yard detectives. He knelt beside the body and went through the victim's pockets in search of a note. He found none. In the bottom right-hand pocket of the waistcoat, he found a piece of silver watch chain – but no watch. In the left-hand pocket of his jacket was an empty blue sugar bag with some crumbs at the bottom. He searched the man's other pockets and found nothing of note. At no time, while he rifled through the dead man's clothing, did Lomasney get blood on his hands. Shining his torch on Walton's neck, he saw 'the blade of a hedging fork and the tine of a two-tine fork were inserted into the man's neck and throat'. Gently pulling at the extreme end of the fork's handle, he found the implement was wedged firmly under the hedge. 'It was obvious then to me,' he later said, 'that there had been foul play, and I said so to Potter and Valender who were standing nearby.'

'Ray,' Lomasney said over his shoulder, 'you had better go home and ring up Stratford Police. Tell them that a man has been murdered and ask them to send someone in authority at once.'

Valender left immediately on his task.

'When was the last time you saw Walton alive?' Lomasney, getting to his feet, asked Potter.

'About ten minutes or a quarter past twelve,' said Potter, 'when I came to feed the cattle and sheep down there.'

Some distance away in the same field, Lomasney could just make out the darkened shapes of several calves. He turned his attention again to the body. The dead man's trousers were unfastened at the top, and the zipper was down. Walton's belt lay across his thighs. The jacket and waistcoat were also unbuttoned; the man's braces appeared torn in the back and unfastened in the front. Lomasney shone his torch in the general vicinity of the body. About 3½ yards from where Walton lay, he saw a walking stick lying near the fence separating Potter and Valender's property. He picked it up and studied it closely in the light of his torch.

'Look at this,' he said, motioning to Potter. 'Blood and hair.'

Indeed, the handled-end of the stick appeared to have been used as a weapon. Seeing the blood seemed to incite some visceral response in Potter.

'It's a devil,' Potter said, 'this happening on my land. What will the public say? You know what they are round Quinton.'

This statement is interesting in light of the rumours and speculation that would eventually swirl about the case. Lomasney does not articulate in his statement what Potter may have meant when he said this, but one might assume the farmer was referring to the superstitious nature of villagers in Upper and Lower Quinton. Potter, a lifelong resident of the area, must have surely grown up hearing stories of local hauntings and witchcraft.

Valender, meanwhile, had hurried back to his house and telephoned the superintendent at Stratford-upon-Avon Police Station.

Other men soon joined Potter, Lomasney, and Harry Peachey – who loitered quietly nearby – in the field. At 7.45 p.m., an Inspector Chester and Sergeant Bailey from the Warwickshire County Constabulary arrived. In their wake, Harry Beasley soon followed with his brother in tow and another local, one Mr Nicholls. While escorting Edith back to the village, away from the nightmare in the field, Beasley had encountered his wife, who had come looking for him. Explaining what had happened, he left Edith in his wife's care and ran to fetch his brother and Mr Nicholls, both of whom lived nearby, for assistance. The two men retrieved a stretcher from an ambulance billeted at The Firs and returned to the field. The growing number of newcomers now seemed to only agitate Potter's discomfort.

'I'm famished,' he said to Lomasney. 'I'll be getting home.'

Lomasney watched Potter retreat into the darkness and head back to The Firs. As Potter left, Dr A.R. McWhinny, who had a private practice in Stratford and was summoned by the police, climbed over the fence and into the field. He would be the first medical expert to examine the body. His notes detail the brutality of the crime:

The body was lying on its left side with the knees and hips in a bent position, and was about one yard from the hedge facing the body and two yards from the hedge running at right angles to this hedge.

There was a gash on the right side of the neck involving the main structures of the neck, and the cut ends of the main vessel and the lacerated trachea (windpipe) could be seen. The blade of a billhook was in situ in the wound. The tip of the blade being at least buried four inches in the tissue at the root of the neck.

The head was turned to the left side and the handle of the billhook lay across the face in a position nearly parallel to the long axis of the body.

In addition to the wound already described, the face was impaled by a pitch fork, one prong of which had entered on either side of the face. On the right side, the point of entrance was just below and in front of the angle of the jaw, and on the left side appeared to be at a somewhat lower level. The handle of the fork had been pressed backwards and the end of the handle was wedged under the cross member of the hedge behind the head, thus anchoring the head to the ground.

The handle of the billhook, which was lying free, was approximately parallel with the handle of the fork.

By now, the field was thrumming with activity. Officers from the Stratford-upon-Avon police department, as well as Detective-Superintendent Alec Spooner of the Warwickshire County Constabulary, who initially led the investigation, had arrived. Police Constable 148 Arthur Nicholls photographed the body, forever capturing the scene in grisly black and white. At 11.30 p.m., Professor James M. Webster of the West Midland Forensic Science Laboratory arrived to examine the body. Webster was a pathologist of high reputation, prompting one newspaper to declare that he was 'as famous as any figure who ever helped solve a crime excepting, perhaps, Sherlock Holmes'.

Shining his torch, Webster could see the ground beneath Walton's head was soaked with blood. The pathologist's first order of business was to remove the hook and fork from the body, which he did with considerable effort. The tines of the pitchfork had been 'plunged into the body a full three-quarters of their length'. Because the fork's handle had been wedged under the bush, the body had to be pushed down slightly in order to free the handle from its entanglement. Kneeling beside the body, Webster discovered Walton's extremities and several of his 'small joints' were free of rigor mortis. Even now, the victim's body retained some of its heat. Webster pulled a thermometer from his case and, 'per rectune,' noted the body temperature at 88 degrees. Taking into account the cold night air, he mentally worked through the calculations of his trade, computing the hourly rate the temperature of one's body drops upon death. The body's overall lack of rigidity and its residual warmth suggested Walton had been dead no more than ten hours.

＊

While Webster examined the body, Detective Inspector Toombs of the Warwickshire County Constabulary made his way through the fields and churchyard to The Firs, the home and farm of Alfred Potter. It was 11 p.m. when Toombs sat at Potter's kitchen table, removed a notebook from his coat pocket, and conducted the investigation's first formal interview. As evident by Toombs's hand-written notes, it was a short interrogation and did not reveal much.

Potter said he went that morning to the College Arms, the pub in Lower Quinton, with another local farmer. He was not there long and left at noon, making a special point to check the time. From the pub, he walked to the lower slope of Meon Hill and entered a field adjacent to the one where Walton was busy trimming the hedges. He could see Walton about 600 yards away and saw the old man still had about 6 to 10 yards of hedge to trim. When the body was discovered later that night, it was clear Walton had trimmed an additional 4 yards of hedge since Potter last saw him that afternoon, which equalled about thirty minutes of work.

'What sort of man was Walton?' asked Toombs.

'He was an inoffensive type,' Potter said, 'but would speak his mind if necessary.'

✳

At 1.45 a.m., Webster ordered the body be removed and taken to the mortuary at General Hospital in Stratford-ipon-Avon, where Webster would perform the autopsy at noon on 15 February. As the body was lifted onto a stretcher, Webster noted the face was covered in blood. There was also a 'considerable amount' of blood on the ground. Valender, who had since returned to the field, helped place the body in a handcart and push it to a waiting ambulance in Upper Quinton. He, too, saw Walton's head 'was covered in blood'. Accounts of the crime published in the years since have claimed Walton's face was frozen in an expression of terror, yet nowhere is such a thing noted in the official case records. Certainly, the people in the field that night never recorded such a detail in their statements – nor did Webster make note of any such facial expression when conducting his autopsy.

In fact, many legitimate details surrounding the circumstances of how Walton's body was found have been lost to fabrication over the years. *The Encyclopedia of Witches, Witchcraft, and Wicca* states Walton's body was 'found lying face-up beneath a willow tree on Meon Hill'. Likewise, in *Devil's Dominion: The Complete Story of Hell and Satanism in the Modern World*, Anthony Masters writes that Walton 'was found, after a day's work, lying underneath a willow tree. There was a look of utter terror on his face. His own pitchfork was driven through his neck, nearly severing his head.' Famed crime and occult historian Colin Wilson references the willow tree in his 1973 book, *The Occult: A History*, as does journalist John Parker in his 1993 tome, *At the Heart of Darkness: Witchcraft, Black Magic and Satanism Today*. As official documentation reveals,

Walton was found lying near a hedge and not beneath a willow tree. So, why has the tree become such a repeated component of the story? According to *The Witches' Craft: The Roots of Witchcraft & Magical Transformation*:

> The Willow tree (Salix alba) is associated with the Underworld and such goddesses as Proserpina and Hectate. The willow was also associated with the serpent, perhaps due to its slender branches. The willow is a tree found near streams, rivers, and swamplands. Its connection with water linked it to the moon and thereby to the moon goddess. It was an ancient practice to place willow branches in the beds of women who were infertile. This was believed to draw mystical serpents that would help with impregnation. From the time of antiquity, the wands used in moon magic were made of willow. It also has a long history for being used to make straps for flagellation. These were used in rites of initiation and purification, as well as sex-magic rituals incorporating pain and pleasure. A length of willow was also traditionally used to bind together the materials for a Witch's broom, the willow being sacred to Hectate.

Another claim made in subsequent accounts about the killing regards the removal of the pitchfork. In his statement to Scotland Yard, Webster said he pulled the fork free of Walton's body and that it took some effort. More than a handful of published sources since then have claimed the pitchfork was plunged so deeply into Walton's prostrate form, it took the might of two uniformed officers to pull the implement free. Nowhere in the official case files is this assertion supported.

It's believed by many that Charles Walton's death was a ritual sacrifice. The violent yet particular way in which he died, claim such believers, suggest that black magic was at play. They point to the ancient Anglo-Saxon practice known as 'stacung' (sticking) – stabbing one's enemy with a pin or thorn and praying the wound causes death – often inflicted upon those believed to be witches. The method did have certain drawbacks, for it's difficult to plunge a thorn into someone's anatomy and then stand over their writhing form and pray for their death. Nevertheless, in early times, 'stacung' proved an effective way of getting rid of one's enemy. 'As the Anglo-Saxons were very reckless in the infliction of wounds, and as the spikes were inserted vigorously in the most tender parts of the person, the incantation was commonly successful, and the victim perished, in their opinion of the curse, but more probably of the wounds.' In the case of Charles Walton, however, the victim's own pitchfork had been used in place of a pin or thorn. As further proof of some sort of sacrifice, many accounts point out the date of the murder – 14 February – and the fact Walton's blood was left to be absorbed by the ground, a practice believed by some to return life to dead soil. Valentine's Day, according to multiple published works on the case, was the day ancient Druids offered a blood-sacrifice to Mother Earth in exchange for a healthy crop season. Although citing a lack of evidence to support such notions, *The Encyclopedia of Witches, Witchcraft, and Wicca* states:

> The crops of 1944 had been poor, and the spring of 1945 did not look promising, either. Walton was known to harness huge toads to toy ploughs and send them running into the fields. In 1662 a Scottish witch, Isobel Gowdie, confessed to doing the same thing in order to blast the crops. Perhaps someone thought Walton was using witchcraft to blast his neighbour's crops. Significantly, Walton's blood had been allowed to drain into the ground. According to old beliefs, a witch's power could be neutralised by 'blooding'. Many accused witches bled to death from cutting and slashing, usually done to the forehead. The practice was done in certain parts of England from the 16th century up to 19th century.

To claim the killer 'allowed' Walton's blood to be absorbed by the ground is a stretch. The old man's throat had been slashed three times with a billhook, severing veins and arteries; the tines of a pitchfork had pinned his head to the ground. Naturally, such wounds would result in the spilling of a lot of blood, which would seep into the ground whether the killer wanted it to or not.

✳

There was little more police could do that night. Having helped with the body's removal, Lomasney returned to the field and watched the other detectives and officers leave. He was soon left alone in the cold, swirling dark to guard the crime scene. He remained on duty until relieved at 3 a.m. by War Reserve Constable Harris. Two hours later, Police Constable John West relieved Harris. The cold and boredom were the two biggest challenges facing West that morning. All was quiet through the dark hours, except the rustling of dead branches in the wind and the occasional sound of a farm animal somewhere in the night.

Shortly after 7 a.m., the first grey light of dawn began to reveal itself in the east, pleasing the constable, for the night-time temperature had been bitter. As the pale winter sun slowly began its climb, West saw a man walking in the field alongside the hedge Walton had been cutting. When the man was no more than a few yards from where Walton had been found, West raised his hand.

'Good morning,' he said. 'Don't go near there.'

'Good morning,' the man said. 'It's been a bit of a frost ain't it?'

'Yes,' West replied. 'It was very sharp an hour ago. Are you the farmer?'

'Yes. My name's Potter; I'm the one who found him. The man's niece thought it funny that Walton had not come home. She went to look for him and came to the farm with Mr Beasley, and we all went to look for him. Me and Mr Beasley was just in front going up the hill, and I saw him. I told Mr Beasley to send the niece back, and I went over to him.'

As Potter spoke, he kept staring at the spot where Walton's body was found. The grass, wet with morning condensation, was stained with Walton's blood. West had not asked Potter to elaborate on the previous night's grim discovery – the man just seemed compelled to share his story. As he continued staring at the bloodstained grass, he said something that would become a focus point of the investigation.

'I didn't touch him,' he told West, 'but I did just put my fingers on the stale of the pitchfork.'

Why Potter never mentioned touching the pitchfork to Lomasney at the crime scene or when he gave his brief statement to Toombs is a mystery. West said nothing and allowed Potter to continue rambling.

'I shouted to someone in the next field to fetch the police,' he said. 'PC Lomasney arrived and examined him. He was all right earlier on when I came up to the cattle. I saw him from over the other field.'

Potter paused and surveyed the surrounding scenery.

'These blasted Italians are poaching all over the place, and it might be one of them,' he said, referring to the Italian inmates of a POW camp in the nearby village of Long Marston. Although technically prisoners, they seemed free to leave the camp whenever they wanted and were often sited walking the slopes of Meon Hill or strolling the nearby lanes. Potter rifled through his pockets for something and pulled out a pack of Player's cigarettes. He offered one to West, who accepted. Potter offered the constable a light and asked if West had been on duty all night.

'No,' West said. 'I'm a relief man.'

Potter said something non-committal and took a deep draw on his cigarette. His eyes again rested on the place where Walton fell. He made another comment about the weather.

'Well,' he said after a moment of brief contemplation, 'I better get some work done.'

Potter bid West a good day and walked back to his farm.

✳

The mortuary at General Hospital in Stratford-upon-Avon, with its white tiles and shining instruments, smelled of antiseptic and formaldehyde. Dressed in a leather apron, Webster stripped the corpse and, with some effort, straightened the crooked form on the metal table. Rigor mortis was now present throughout the entire body. Under the glare of the mortuary lights, it was evident a life in the fields, performing manual labour, had benefitted Walton's physique. Although he appeared to have been well nourished, his body was wiry and corded with muscle. With a sponge, Webster wiped away the dry blood and commenced his external examination of the body, noting: 'The deceased was a little, rather bent old man, with a certain amount of curvature of the spine.' Much has been made of the injuries Walton suffered during the attack. Subsequent accounts of the crime have stated the killer repeatedly carved the sign of the cross into Walton's body. The official case file, however, not once mentions any disfigurement of this kind. Here, taken directly from Webster's autopsy report, are the external injuries noted on Walton's body:

1. There were four large bruises on the back of the right hand and back of the right forearm. These were definitely ante-mortem, and the blood had not clotted.
2. There was a small abrasion on the point of the right elbow.
3. There was flap laceration on the back of the index finger of the left hand, such as could have been caused by the old man

defending himself against a cutting instrument. There were no injuries to the palms of the hands.

4. On the top of the left shoulder there were superficial abrasions and bruises, such as could have been caused by the hayfork, which I saw.
5. There were seven lacerated wounds of the scalp situated on the back and top of the head. None of these wounds led down to the bone. Later in the post-mortem, I ascertained that these wounds were superimposed upon deep-seated bruises in the scalp.
6. On palpitation, I ascertained that the left clavicle had been completely severed from the sternum.
7. By palpitation, I ascertained that there were several ribs broken on the left side and later in the dissection I ascertained that the ribs that were broken were the second ribs and the sixth to the ninth ribs inclusive. There was free extravasation of blood in the region of the fractured ribs.
8. The main wound in the neck extended from a point about 1in below the point of the chin down to the suprasternal notch. It was obvious that this hole, which measured 4¼in by 3½in had been made by more than one slash. The tissues on the front of the neck were grossly cut about, and there was a free communication between this hole and the left pleural cavity.

On either side of the slash were the puncture wounds caused by hayfork prongs. Webster reached for a nearby tray and picked up his scalpel. He made a large Y-shaped incision, which ran down from both shoulders to just below the navel. There was no ingested blood in the stomach, though Webster did find the remains of a recently ingested meal, which had included currants. It was no doubt the slice of cake prepared and packed by Edith. Webster picked up a bone saw and cut through the rib cage. The heart appeared to be 'remarkably healthy for an old man of this age'. The lungs revealed a moderate degree of bronchitis but had otherwise been healthy in life. The left tine of the hayfork had punctured the left lung.

Peering into the chest cavity, Webster saw the left clavicle had been completely severed from the sternum. The pectoral muscle was severely bruised, and the second, sixth, and ninth ribs were broken. Moving up the body, he began to dissect the neck and saw just how deep the fatal blow had struck. All the major muscles and vessels in the neck had been slashed. The blade had severed the thyroid gland and the longitudinal ligament of the spine on the left-hand side. The hayfork tines had punctured the pleural cavity. The trachea and upper respiratory tract, upon internal inspection, revealed the killer had actually delivered multiple blows to Walton's neck. Webster wrote:

> These were in three sections, a part consisting of the epiglottis, a second part consisting of part of the hyoid bone and the thyroid cartilage, including the vocal cords; a third part consisting of the trachea. This division of the respiratory tract clearly showed that three separate and distinct blows by a cutting instrument had been delivered.

The esophagus had also been completely severed. Removing the skullcap, Webster saw no trauma to the skull or brain. None of the lacerations on the back and top of the scalp had penetrated down to the bone.

The autopsy done, Webster made note of his verdict:

> This had been a remarkably healthy old man for his age. The cause of death is quite clear. He died from shock and hemorrhage due to grave injuries to the neck and chest. These injuries had been caused by two types of weapon, namely, a cutting weapon and a stabbing weapon such as the two weapons I found in situ in the field. Further, the cutting weapon had been wielded at least three times and with great violence. The old man had defended himself, as shown by the cut upon the left hand and the bruises on the back of the right hand and forearm. Death had occurred in my opinion somewhere between 1 p.m. and 2 p.m. on the 14th February, 1945.

How did the supposed carving of the cross become part of the Walton case folklore? Contemporary newspaper accounts of the slaying not once reported the killer leaving a cross-shaped mark on his victim. Of course, the police would be unlikely to share that information with reporters. Perhaps, then, local word-of-mouth – the rumour mill – is to blame.

The fabrication is echoed in one case study after another. 'Walton had been pinned to the ground with his own pitchfork. The prongs had passed through his neck and penetrated a full six inches into the ground,' states one account. 'It needed two policemen to pull it clear. In addition, the sign of the cross had been sliced into the victim's chest with the blade of the billhook.' From yet another: 'The body of the old man was badly mutilated ... His throat had been cut and his chest had been slashed with a crude sign of the cross.' And another, this one with an additional flourish: 'A cross-shaped wound had been slashed on his chest with the bill hook, which was stuck into his ribs. Walton's face was contorted in terror. A few days later, a black dog was found hanged on Meon Hill.' As with other facets of the case that have become part of the public record, official case files make no reference to a black dog being hanged on Meon Hill shortly after the crime. Nevertheless, the authors of the aforementioned accounts should not be blamed for publishing misinformation. Carved crosses and spectral hounds have been written about so many times in conjunction with Walton's killing, they've come to be accepted as fact.

The autopsy complete, Webster sent Walton's walking stick, fingernails, and clothing to the West Midland Forensic Science Laboratory in Birmingham for forensic analysis. That same day, Warwickshire police returned en force to the scene of the crime. Armed with metal detectors, cameras, magnifying glasses, shovels, and a myriad other tools necessary for the searching, sifting, and sorting of evidence, officers spread out through the killing field – and the surrounding area – looking for anything that might point investigators in the right direction. The very setting of the crime posed its own unique challenges. The site of the killing had been exposed to the elements all night, meaning temperature and condensation had most likely corrupted or destroyed any trace evidence. Determining the size and boundaries of an outdoor crime scene is no easy task. Unlike a house or flat, there was no specific point of entry or escape that might yield evidence. The surrounding fields were also searched but turned up nothing beneficial.

While officers searched the lower slopes of Meon Hill, other investigators knocked on doors in Lower Quinton, finding out what they could about Walton. No, said one villager after another, he was not on bad terms with anyone. Yes, he kept to himself but was pleasant to those he met in passing. To village residents, in their bucolic setting of thatched roofs, rolling fields, and winding lanes in the heart of England, the police presence and the questions being asked were most disconcerting. As one recent study on the case notes, residents surely disliked 'stern-eyed cops striding from house to house, asking whether they might happen to know of any crazed, pitchfork-wielding neighbour capable of directing a maniacal battering against a frail, elderly man. Surely, news of this kind would not enhance their social profile or increase the market value of their properties.'

Edith Walton, still in a state of shock, detailed for police Walton's final morning at the cottage. She was shown an inventory list of items found on his body:

1. Cardigan
a. Left pocket: Red handkerchief.
b. Right pocket: Three pieces of string and a foot of sock.

2. Jacket
a. Right pocket: Whetstone and piece of rope with hook attached, three pieces of string.

3. Waistcoat
a. Left bottom pocket: Foot of sock and pocketknife.
b. Left top pocket: Length of watch chain and small tin containing four gun licenses.

4. Blue Overall Trousers
a. Right pocket: Piece of rag.
b. Left pocket: Receipt No. 20 for 8/-.

Missing, said Edith, was the metal pocket watch her uncle always wore. She described it as 'a plain white metal watch, snap case at the back, white enamel face, English numerals, keyless'. The dial featured the name of the watchmaker, 'Edgar Jones, Stratford-on-Avon.' The missing watch aside, the initial police canvas turned up nothing. By day's end, it was clear local authorities – unaccustomed to handling such cases – required outside help. At 10.55 p.m. on Thursday,

15 February, the deputy chief constable of the Warwickshire Constabulary wired the following message to Scotland Yard:

> The Chief Constable has asked me to get the assistance of Scotland Yard to assist in a brutal case of murder that took place yesterday. The deceased is a man named Charles Walton, age 75 [sic], and he was killed with an instrument known as a slash hook. The murder was either committed by a madman or one of the Italian prisoners who are in a camp nearby. The assistance of an Italian interpreter would be necessary, I think. Dr Webster states the deceased was killed between 1 and 2 p.m. A metal watch is missing from the body. It is being circulated.

At 12.10 a.m. on 16 February, the chief constable of the Criminal Investigation Division at Scotland Yard wired back his response:

> Chief Inspector Fabian and another officer will leave London tomorrow for Leamington Spa. The time of arrival of the train they are catching will be notified to you in due course.

2

A DETECTIVE'S EDUCATION

Today, it's hard to imagine a police officer becoming a household name, the subject of a television programme and multiple movies, or a sort of national icon symbolising the pursuit of justice. Such a notion seems to speak of a simpler time, when violent crime – particularly murder – still had the power to shock. Scotland Yard Superintendent Robert Honey Fabian, otherwise known as 'Fabian of the Yard', worked his trade when the exploits of Scotland Yard detectives made front pages and sold newspapers almost daily.

Growing up, Fabian never put much thought into becoming a police officer. He was born on 31 January 1901 in the south-east London district of Ladywell. Unsure what direction to take in life, he followed his father's career path and went into engineering. At the age of 12, after completing elementary school, he was sent by his parents to the Borough Polytechnic to acquire the necessary skills to become an engineering draftsman. He tackled his studies with the bare minimum of enthusiasm and, in his opinion, did quite poorly on his final exams – or so he thought. His scores were sufficient enough to land him a succession of drafting jobs, all of which promised a lifetime of sitting in front of a drawing table working on various schematics – a fate he quickly determined was not for him. The monotony of the same routine day-in and day-out seemed suffocating. In an office environment, he later remarked, he fit in 'about as well as a recluse at holiday camp. I could draw well enough, but the long hours on a high stool and the lack of fresh air irked me.

I was eager to get out into life and deal with people rather than with things.'

The dull nature of the work wore him down. He worried life was passing him by with few experiences to show for it. Making the situation all the more dire was the lack of other career possibilities. His parents had scrimped and saved to send him to the polytechnic. To turn his back on his work in pursuit of something else would, in his mind, have been akin to letting them down. These thoughts weighed heavily on his mind, as he returned home from work one evening in 1921. Entering the house, he found his parents entertaining a friend in the living room. The visitor was a gentleman of immense size and seemed giant-like to Fabian who, at 5 feet 10 inches tall, was not wanting in the height department. The man introduced himself as Frederick Rolfe, a local police inspector. Fabian joined his parents and Rolfe for tea and listened as the family friend discussed some of his adventures on the police force. Until this moment, Fabian had equated being a policeman to something out of a Conan Doyle story. 'Like most youngsters of my generation,' he later wrote, 'I imagined myself in a deerstalker hat and tweed cape, puffing at a curled pipe as I examined footprints with an outsize magnifying glass.'

Rolfe's stories of walking the beat, collaring crooks, and learning the fine science of detection, cast aside in Fabian's mind any romantic notion he may have had of police work. The grittiness and unpredictability of it appealed to him. Surely, working the streets would expose him to people and experiences in a way no office environment ever could. He questioned Rolfe more about his line of work and went to bed that evening excited. An escape from the drawing table and the dull routine of an office job had revealed itself when all seemed hopeless. Not long thereafter, Fabian approached Rolfe and asked for his help in joining the police force. Happy to oblige, Rolfe sat with Fabian and helped him complete a job application, which they submitted to the Lewisham Police Station.

'I remember what struck me most at that first glimpse of the inside of a police station was how different the men looked without their helmets on,' Fabian later recalled. 'They became individuals instead of just impassive arms of the law. There was also the indefinable police station smell, that even after twenty-eight years of it I can never properly recall – a mixture of scrubbing soap, disinfectant and typewriter ribbons.'

The place thrummed with activity; a stark contrast to the staid office environment to which Fabian had become accustomed. Fabian handed his application to the desk sergeant, who eyed the young man up and down. In a somewhat haughty voice, the sergeant said there was no shortage of young men eager to join the ranks of the Metropolitan Police Service. Fabian, however, would be given as fair a chance as any of the other adventure seekers. The sergeant called to an officer, who led Fabian into a room to be weighed and measured. '5 feet 10 inches, tall enough,' Fabian later wrote in his memoirs. '10 stone 4 pounds, not so good.'

Fabian left the station unsure of his chances but certain in the knowledge he had found his calling. The police station's vibrancy had stirred something in him. How wonderful it would be to face each morning knowing he would not be anchored to a desk. How could he ever return to the drafting table now and the oppressive silence and boredom of a corporate office? He returned home and tried, over the next several days, to keep his mind occupied. An official form arrived in the mail the following week that detailed specific qualifications for police work. All applicants had to be of 'British birth and pure British descent,' between the ages of 20 and 27, be able to read, write, and have a basic knowledge of maths. Yes, all this applied to Fabian, which meant the next hurdle to clear was an in-depth physical. Much to his relief, he received the all clear and was ordered to report for duty at 2 p.m. on 17 May 1921.

The man who would become one of Britain's most celebrated detectives began his career as a police constable assigned to the old Vine Street Police Station, situated behind the Piccadilly Hotel. The station itself was situated behind the Piccadilly Hotel. Showing up at the assigned date and time, Police Constable Fabian – warrant number 111858 – was issued his stiff blue uniform and helmet, and shown where to change. He was placed under the supervision of an older constable, who told him all beginners started out on the night beat. Tugging at the collar of his dress blue shirt, Fabian theorised the nocturnal patrols allowed rookies 'to get used to the uniform in the dark!' That night, supervised by his mentor, he walked his first beat. The senior constable showed Fabian where the various beats began and ended, pointing out the distinguishing landmarks of each, including pubs, churches, the homes of local doctors, and alarm posts to summon the fire department if needed. As they walked the darkened streets, past quiet storefronts and lonely doorways, the senior constable shared with Fabian the knowledge he had acquired following years pounding the pavement.

'On the beat an officer should normally walk the regulation 2½mph – if he is hurrying, he is probably after someone or more likely going home to supper,' Fabian later recalled:

> Properly carried out, patrol duty is not half so dull as you might imagine. The most ordinary looking street can to the practiced eye be of absorbing interest. Each doorway, shadow at a window, hurried footstep or meaningful glance may have a tale to tell. There is, of course, a great deal of luck in patrolling. It is largely a matter of going down the right street at the right moment – as someone once said to me, deciding which are the lucky streets is what counts.

That first night, he found the responsibility of his new profession weighing heavily on his shoulders. There was so much to take in; so many places to learn and procedures to remember. At a drawing table, if you made a mistake, you simply took a rubber, erased the errant line, and started over. On the streets, a mistake might mean death. He would have to familiarise himself with various neighbourhoods and the inhabitants of each. Making friends on the beat, the elder constable said, ensured an extra set of eyes were watching things when you weren't around. Each successive night Fabian spent on patrol nurtured his confidence. He soon found he no longer felt self-conscious in his uniform, but empowered. Before long, he was walking the beat on his own and familiarising himself with shopkeepers and publicans.

'Walking the streets of the West End – the murky ones as well as the bright ones – one felt, as I have frequently thought, like a gamekeeper who takes over an estate of crowded coverts and woodlands,' Fabian once wrote. 'One night, you would walk down Frith Street, say, and everything would be exactly as it was the night before. Tomorrow, there would be a new face on the corner – some pert, hard-eyed girl with a sexily painted mouth and slightly foreign look about her.'

Fabian would make a point of chatting up this new arrival on his beat. Generally, a girl's pimp would emerge from a darkened doorway upon seeing a copper and make a formal introduction. The working girls and their pimps – along with other shady denizens of the West End – would all soon get to know Fabian. He would, in time, develop a reputation for not only his tough, street-smart demeanour – but also, his reciprocity. As long as such individuals treated Fabian with the respect worthy of his uniform, he would always do his utmost to treat them fairly.

When not on duty, Fabian lived with other young constables in police-provided housing at 42 Beak Street in Soho. Each man had his own cubicle, measuring a cramped 'eight feet by seven feet and separated by a partition seven feet high'. The accommodations seemed more akin to a prison cell, with their small cot, chair, single shelf, a box in which to store one's helmet, and a flap attached to the wall that pulled down on a hinge to form a chair. The only decorating permitted in each cube was a framed picture on the shelf of perhaps a girlfriend or family member. Privacy was a rare commodity, as the lock on each cubicle door could be operated from the inside and out, meaning anyone could intrude upon your personal space. Despite what seemed to be a rather spartan existence, Fabian and the other men enjoyed the lifestyle. 'It was a good life in most ways,' Fabian remembered, 'and we had more than our share of fun even if the pay was only £3 less stoppages.'

✳

Fabian was dedicated to the job. Even after completing a shift, or on his off days, he routinely patrolled the streets. One evening, he allowed his future wife Winnie to accompany him on one of his off-duty patrols. Nothing seemed out of the ordinary until they spotted two young men paying very close attention to some parked cars. The way they nervously glanced around before peering through a car window immediately piqued Fabian's curiosity. With Winnie at his side, he followed the two men to Sloane Square. He felt confident, should the need arise, to apprehend both men at once. To keep in shape, he boxed on Tuesday nights and supplemented his pugilistic know-how with ju-jitsu classes. The arts of surveillance and following, however, were still new to the young officer. Once, while shadowing a suspected thief, the suspect simply turned around and handed

Fabian his business card. 'This might save you time,' the man said, leaving a stunned Fabian to ponder what he did wrong. Fortunately, he proved a quick study. Instead of trailing close behind and risk being spotted – or trailing too far back and risk losing his prey – Fabian learned it was more effective to track them from the 'opposite side of the road, often by watching their reflection in shop windows'.

In Sloane Square, the two men busied themselves, scurrying from one parked car to another in search of valuables. From one vehicle, they began lifting two rolled-up rugs. Fabian told Winnie to go and find a uniformed constable. He watched her run off before approaching the two men, his nerves buzzing like live wires. His training had taught him to never use more force than necessary. It was better, a senior officer once told him, to be reprimanded for injuring a suspect than letting the suspect go – or being injured oneself. As luck would have it, the two thieves – struggling with the rugs – had their hands too full to resist. Fabian made his arrest and waited for Winnie to return with a constable. The incident was a major confidence booster for the young officer. Before long he was making arrests on a routine basis, hauling in the disruptive drunk and breaking up the occasional fight.

He earned the attention of his superiors the following year, 1922, when he was called upon to put his drawing skills to use. The Vice Squad was planning to raid a Soho night club where various illicit activities routinely took place. Fabian was asked to familiarise himself with the club and make a detailed drawing of its layout. Fabian's work, and the success of the resulting raid, earned him a temporary attachment to the Vice Squad. He now spent his shifts watching 'clubs, brothels, betting houses and other establishments of doubtful character'. As a result of his new duties, Fabian got to know a number of underworld types, from hustlers to gangsters, to the working girls who strolled the streets. He was surprised to find the ladies were 'very independent' types, many of whom maintained nicely furnished West End apartments for the sole purpose of conducting business. When finished for the day, many would retire to their homes in the suburbs where, amongst oblivious neighbours, they lived a seemingly respectable life. One woman in particular made an impression on the young copper. 'Battling Annie' balanced her 16-stone frame on a pair of 5-inch heels and took it upon herself to keep other Mayfair working girls in line. If she spotted another woman being too obvious while soliciting business or trying to steal a client away from a competitor, she swooped in and would deliver a vicious beating. For the most part, he found the women possessed a bawdy, good-natured sense of humour and stuck to their line of work for the money alone.

He enjoyed forging relationships with members of London's underworld. Associating with criminal elements was a key to the Vice Squad's success. It allowed officers to cultivate informants while also giving them insight as to the workings of the criminal mind. 'I soon realised that if I was to beat the crook,' wrote Fabian, 'I would have to try and see his point of view, study his methods and follow the reasoning of his warped mind.' Fabian, however, did not see the world in simple terms of black and white. While he had little sympathy for hardened criminals, he understood one's circumstances could force them onto a crooked path. If he knew a suspect had a hard upbringing, or was pushed by a tragic turn of events onto the wrong side of the law, he felt such information should be put forward in a court of law. Indeed, as he advanced in his career, he would often be called to testify against those he arrested. When criminals he put away were eventually released from prison, he'd make a point of giving them a fiver and words of encouragement. Such kindness, he believed, went a long way in keeping one-time convicts out of prison. The underworld, he quickly learned, was a squalid, dirty place where one wrong look or a simple word uttered could mean violent death. By 1923, after two years on the force, he decided to apply to the Metropolitan Police Service's Criminal Investigation Division. He passed the necessary exams and soon made his 'first appearance on the street, absurdly self-conscious, in plain clothes'.

The Criminal Investigation Division, or CID, succeeded the Met's Detective Branch, which was reorganised following a notorious police scandal in 1877. That year, two English conmen – Harry Benson and William Kurr – tricked a rich Parisian woman out of £30,000 in a scam involving horseracing bets. Scotland Yard was promptly called in to investigate. Much to the chagrin of detectives working the case, Benson and Kurr always seemed to be one step ahead of investigators, avoiding arrest with frustrating regularity. When the men were finally captured, it was discovered Kurr had been slipping payments to a Scotland Yard inspector for the past several years in exchange for words of warning whenever the police were closing in. The inspector – and two other high-level officers aware of the corruption – were arrested, tried, and sent to prison for two years. The Detective Branch, permanently marked by the scandal, was reorganised into the CID.

Fabian's stomping ground was Soho, which, in those days, was a far cry from the tourist attraction it is today. Its theatres and chic restaurants stood alongside brothels and gambling dens. With Oxford Street to the north, Piccadilly Circus and Leicester Square to the south, Charing Cross Road to the east and Regent Street to the west, Soho was its own little world. Night clubs and houses of ill-repute were the main draws to Soho at that time, and it was Fabian's job to become familiar with all of them – to learn where London's smugglers, gangsters, and other criminal elements conducted their dark trade. Fabian was well suited for the job. He was still young and learning the ropes, as such, he hadn't been around much and was still a stranger to many being targeted by the CID's Vice Squad, headquartered at Vine Street Police Station. The more seasoned investigators, by contrast, were known by sight and reputation, making it all but impossible to blend in with the city's undesirables. It was Fabian's job, then, to be a 'ghost', to move unobserved through Soho's smoky dens, with his mouth shut but his 'eyes and ears open'. In such places, Fabian was an angel among devils. 'I doubt if any young man in London looked less like a policeman than I did at the time,' Fabian wrote. 'Despite three years' duty as a Metropolitan constable, I still gave the impression of a rather innocent youth. Perhaps the fact that I did not smoke or drink had something to do with it?'

Slowly, but surely, he began to notice things: an envelope thick with money exchanging hands beneath a table, an illegal card game in a back room, stolen goods being hawked in an alley. Information obtained by Fabian resulted in raids on a number of clubs and brothels, closing many such establishments permanently. Every takedown, every bust, was all part of his larger police education; another stepping-stone toward the senior ranks and high-profile cases. It was a learning experience Fabian thoroughly enjoyed, for police work had become an all-consuming passion. It wasn't merely the unpredictable nature of the work that appealed to him, but the sense he was accomplishing something worthwhile. He was also doing what he had always wanted to do, dealing with people and living life – not just a mundane day-to-day existence behind a desk, but a gritty, exciting, and dangerous reality.

Despite what his superiors may have thought, however, Fabian's youthfulness didn't always mean he passed unnoticed. One night, while keeping an eye on a gang of French mobsters in an underground club behind Frith Street, Fabian sat at the bar nursing a drink. Some of the French girls, noticing his refreshment of choice, teased him with a new nickname: 'The Little Water Drinker'. Much to Fabian's slight amusement, the name stuck. 'I found it following me from haunt to haunt in Soho,' he later wrote. 'I was becoming known (though not yet as a detective).' Meanwhile, on the force, he was becoming known for the passion with which he tackled the job. For several months, the Vice Squad had been keeping an eye on the Quadrant Club in Regent Street, a place where one could partake in various illicit pleasures. Fabian had spent a considerable amount of time at the club and relaying intelligence back to his superiors.

The Vice Squad scheduled a raid on the club for one evening in May 1924 with Fabian in charge of the operation. The plan hatched by Fabian called for raiding the premises from above, taking advantage of a skylight that was routinely left open, for neither the front nor back entrances of the club allowed for a surprise approach. Next door to the club, a new building was going up. Fabian, with three officers as backup, entered the construction site and made his way up to the building's roof, climbing the steel scaffolding. It was warm for May and the effort made him sweat. Reaching the unfinished roof, the raiding party carefully made its way across a plank walkway to the roof of the Quadrant. The men trod lightly, desperate to maintain the element of surprise. Mopping his brow, Fabian was pleased to see the club owner had propped the Quadrant's fanlight open about three inches. When Fabian tried to open it all the way, however, he discovered it was locked in place. As the three other officers watched, Fabian strained to dislodge the fanlight and lost his footing when his heel slipped on the roof's moss-covered surface. Waving his arms frantically to regain his balance, he fell forward and crashed through the fanlight. As splintered glass rained down, Fabian grabbed a red curtain hanging from a rod in the ceiling, near the fanlight opening. He clung desperately to the thick cloth before it gave way and sent him tumbling to the floor. He landed with a bone-jarring thud on his back in a shimmering pool of glass shards, the impact knocking the air from his lungs.

Bruised and struggling to catch his breath, Fabian picked himself up, wincing at the pain in his hands. Both palms, sliced by glass, were slick with blood.

'You all right?' shouted one of the officers, still up on the roof.

'All right,' Fabian called back, finding his feet.

He looked around and realised he was in the lady's room. Fortunately, the facilities were unoccupied. Having recovered from the fall, he called up through the shattered fanlight and told the officers on the roof to signal the men at street level he was about to unlock the front door. He made his way to the cloakroom exit and stepped out onto the stairs, only to see two of the club's more brutish-looking waiters – believing a thief had just gained entry through the cloakroom fanlight – rushing in his direction. As the goons closed in, Fabian recalled a move he'd once seen performed in a wrestling ring. Grabbing the large brass door handle to the cloakroom, Fabian pushed up with his arms and swung both legs out in a vicious kick. The two waiters took the full brunt of the attack and crashed back down the stairs. A club member happened to pass by on the floor below just as the two waiters came to rest on the bottom step in a jumble of arms and legs. The member, a man with a reputation for high spending whom Fabian had seen in the club before, looked up the stairs in surprise and saw the bloodied and dishevelled detective.

'Well done, Robert,' the man said, as though congratulating Fabian on a lucky roll of the dice or a good poker hand.

Fabian nodded in acknowledgement and made his way down the stairs, stepping carefully over the human wreckage. He made his way to the club's front door, ignoring the puzzled stares of members, who undoubtedly wondered what such a mess of a man was doing in a place like this. No sooner had Fabian opened the front door and let a swarm of officers in did the stunned clientele have their answer.

The Quadrant raid established Fabian's reputation as a man of action – an officer unafraid to take risks. Throughout his career he would prove more than eager to match brawn – as well as wits – with London's criminal denizens.

✻

Before long, he had enrolled in the Detective Training School in Hendon. Students, applying their knowledge of criminal investigation, were called upon to solve staged crimes of various types. The cast of characters one might experience on a case – from low-level gangland enforcers to fast-talking card sharks or smugglers – were also discussed, as were the methods these individuals might employ to conduct their type of business. While interesting, Fabian noted the training was 'of little value without previous practical experience on the beat, in the pubs, in the cafés, the race-courses and other places where crooks love to go'.

It was about this time Fabian went up against a new kind of criminal. A series of high-profile burglaries had recently mystified the detectives at Vine Street. Money and jewels had been stolen from a number of prominent London residences. Once a week, a new break-in was reported. The culprit seemed to be gaining entrance to houses by accessing windows on the third and fourth floors, a task one could not easily accomplish without a ladder. Within a five-week period, £30,000 in valuables had been pilfered from homes along Park Lane. Fabian – then a 'probationer-detective' – and a fellow detective-in-training took it upon themselves to try and crack the case. Studying a map of the area where the burglaries had occurred, the two young upstarts guessed the thief would next target mansions near the Ritz corner. The two men decided to keep an eye on Wimborne House, one of the largest houses in the area. They took up positions on a chilly night in the shrubbery at the back of the house. There, they waited several hours, cramped and uncomfortable, their breath crystallising in the frigid air. As the night wore on, the young officers began to wonder if they were wasting their time. What were they doing out here? It wasn't even their case.

As the thought of a hot cup of tea threatened to lure Fabian from his hiding place, he heard something. Peering over the shrubbery he used to conceal himself, he saw a shadowy figure moving quickly through the garden. The intruder was 'quick, agile as a cat'. Fabian watched as the figure leapt with graceful ease and cleared the high fence separating the house from the garden. Fabian's partner broke cover and moved quietly toward the house. From his vantage point, Fabian could see the upper floors of the house and watched with a begrudging sense of awe as the intruder seemingly appeared out of nowhere and leapt from one window balcony to another. Just as quickly as he had appeared, the nimble stranger – having silently pried open a window – disappeared into the house's dark interior. Neither young detective had ever seen a person move with such athleticism. Fabian's partner alerted the homeowners, who began running through the house and turning on all the lights. When they got to the room the thief had entered, they found the large mahogany door barricaded from the inside. Later, they would discover the thief had jammed the door shut with a small wooden wedge. As the sound of banging doors and excited voices filtered from the house into the garden, Fabian saw the thief re-emerge onto the balcony.

Now, thought Fabian, was his chance to catch him – but the thief had other plans. Instead of descending into the garden, he leapt to a neighbouring balcony, covering a distance of 9 feet. Another running jump launched him from the balcony to the roof of the house next door. And, with that, he was gone.

A small army of uniformed constables and plainclothes detectives arrived on the scene and began scouring the neighbourhood, to no avail. The senior officer, an inspector, was less than thrilled with Fabian's proactive approach. Why, the inspector demanded, had Fabian not informed him of his plan to lie in wait for the thief? More officers could have been assigned to the surveillance operation to prevent the very thing that had just happened. Fabian had no answer – he couldn't even provide an adequate description of the suspect. He had only seen the man in silhouette. The only distinguishing feature he had been able to make out in the ambient light coming from the house was a glistening diamond stud fastened in what appeared to be a dress shirt.

The thief had made off with £2,000 in jewellery. The manhunt continued well into the morning. Standing in the cold light of day on the balcony from which the thief had made his getaway leap, Fabian noticed a faint footprint on the balcony's white, marble edge – a print so pointed in the toe, it could have been made by a woman's high-heel. Another footprint was discovered on the roof of the neighbouring house. The smooth surface of the tiles revealed a unique pattern to the print, which Fabian recognised as 'the porous tread of crepe soles'. The shoes, being of a type not readily available in your average shoe shop, had most likely been made to order. Fabian immediately set about visiting high-end shoe stores that could cater to such requests. At a shop in Albermarle Street, Fabian flashed his identity card and asked the owner if any male customers in recent months had requested a pair of evening pumps with rubber soles. The owner didn't have to check his orders. He said a client had recently requested such a pair of shoes with very thin, crepe rubber soles. The owner had told the customer shoes of this type would not be practical for everyday wear, but the customer was insistent.

The owner pulled out a leather-bound order book and began flipping through its pages. He finally found the desired entry and turned the book around so Fabian could read it: 'R. Radd, 52, Half Moon Street. Five guineas – paid.' What luck, thought Fabian, jotting down the address. He made his way to Half Moon Street but quickly discovered the house numbers stopped at 42. Mr Radd – if that was even his real name – had provided a fake address. Far from admitting defeat, Fabian decided to canvas the neighbourhood's bars and clubs. 'Those were the days of evening clothes for gentlemen in London's West End,' Fabian later wrote, 'so my laundry bill became staggering.'

For the next several weeks, Fabian put on the best his wardrobe had to offer and spent his evenings in search of his prey. The clubs and bars in the district were high-class affairs and not exactly Fabian's scene. Pulling at the stiff, white collar of his dress shirt as he entered the Range Club one evening, he was thinking a pint at The Prospect of Whitby at Wapping Wall or The Mitre in Ely Place, off Holborn Circus, would be more preferable to another night spent in the company of high rollers. He was very much aware of his polished shoes when he entered the club, for they clicked loudly on the equally shiny parquet floor. As he made his way towards the bar, a gentleman heading for the door walked past him. The flash of a diamond pin in the man's lapel caught Fabian's attention – as did the fact the man's shoes made absolutely no sound at all. Fabian cast his eyes downward and noticed the man's leather shoes ended in a very pointy toe.

Fabian waited for the man to leave the club then followed him outside. From a distance, he watched the gentleman walk down the street. Fabian tailed the man down a side street off Half Moon Street and watched him disappear into No. 43. Pointy shoes and a diamond pin were not enough to warrant an arrest. He took a taxi to Scotland Yard headquarters, then housed in a red-brick building of gothic design on the Embankment, and made his way up to the Criminal Records Office. The CRO was a vital weapon in the detective's arsenal. It housed, according to Fabian, 'the dossier of almost every crook in Europe, their particulars marked down with the help of an intricate filing system. If a man is a burglar, has a deformed foot, a trick of crumbling his table bread into pellets, he will be filed under each of these things and half a dozen besides, as well as by his own name, aliases, height and age.' A review of files turned up nothing on the address. Fabian alerted his supervisors to his recent discovery, prompting the Yard to put a round-the-clock tail on the man. For two days detectives shadowed the suspect's movements with little to show for their efforts. On the third day, they followed him to a café in Hatton Garden, where he met another gentleman. They left the café together and took a taxi to a house in Southgate.

The suspect eventually left the house and returned to his own residence. When detectives knocked on the door of the Southgate address, they came face-to-face with a well-known fence, who admitted to having paid £800 for stolen jewellery. This was all Fabian needed to hear. He immediately made his way to the suspect's flat; 'Delaney' read the name under the door buzzer. Once the landlady had let him into the building, Fabian ran up the stairs to Delaney's flat. He didn't bother knocking but charged right in, surprising the occupant, a slender man of trim and athletic build. He leapt up from his chair and demanded Fabian identify himself; his tone of righteous indignation fading when Fabian demanded to know where Delaney kept the jewellery.

'I suppose it's too much to hope that you gentlemen are burglars,' Delaney said with resigned good humour.

Fabian couldn't help but smile as he shook his head. A search of the flat uncovered the stolen jewels hidden in a bedroom drawer. The £800 was under the mattress. Robert Augustus Delaney was arrested and taken to Scotland Yard, where he revealed his *modus operandi*. Delaney always committed his crimes in immaculate evening dress. Unlike his predecessors in the trade – men like the notorious nineteenth century thief and murderer Charles Peace – who used a collapsible ladder to scale buildings and gain entry – Delaney, with his trim physique and pointy-toed shoes, 'could apparently climb the sheer side of a house'. He used a long blade, not unlike a putty knife, to unfasten window locks. His shoes, as Fabian already knew, were specifically designed to minimise sound. Once he had the loot in hand, he would uncoil four yards of black silk rope from around his waist and descend from the open window. Fabian and the other officers, upon learning of Delaney's methods, couldn't help but be impressed. Scotland Yard would go on to consider Delaney the first modern-day cat burglar. Delaney received a three-year sentence for the Park Lane burglaries and would spend the rest of his life in and out of prison.

Had Fabian not noticed the diamond pin Delaney had been wearing in the Range Club, the burglaries might have gone unsolved. But, like any great detective, Fabian excelled at noticing the small details – the seemingly innocuous item that other people would most likely overlook.

3

FABIAN ARRIVES

In July 1860, Detective-Inspector Jonathan Whicher became the first Scotland Yard officer dispatched to investigate a crime outside London. The case in question, the murder of 3-year-old Saville Kent, rocked Victorian England and would inspire Wilkie Collins in his writing of *The Moonstone* and the flight of Helena Landless in Charles Dickens's *The Mystery of Edwin Drood*.

Between the late-night hours of 29 June and the early morning hours of the following day, Saville was taken from his family's Georgian-style home, Road Hill House, near the Wiltshire village of Road. The boy was found later that morning, in his nightshirt and wrapped in a blood-soaked blanket, lying in the pit beneath the lavatory seat of the outhouse. His throat had been sliced almost to the point of decapitation.

Whicher's theory of the crime was based purely on circumstantial evidence – and questionable evidence at that. He arrested Saville's 16-year-old half-sister, Constance, after discovering one of her three nightdresses had gone missing shortly after the killing. The young girl told Whicher 'the other was lost at the wash the week after the murder'. Whicher believed the girl had destroyed the nightdress because she had bloodied it while taking a blade to the young victim. When the case went to magistrate's court, contrary to stirring public wrath, the defendant garnered widespread sympathy. Although Kent confessed to a priest that she did, indeed, kill the boy, it was believed she was lying to save her father, who many, including

Charles Dickens, believed to be the real killer. She was nevertheless found guilty and sentenced to death. Due to her age at the time of the crime, her sentence was commuted to life. She would eventually serve twenty years in prison. The case, with its many questions and unknown motive, forever tarnished Whicher's reputation.

Despite its less-than-satisfying conclusion, the Murder at Road Hill House would not be the last case to draw Scotland Yard detectives away from the city. In 1907, based on a Home Office assessment, it was recommended Scotland Yard, if asked, should assume command of murder investigations in rural areas:

> The County Police, excluding a few large provincial cities, have no detective forces. They deal well enough with the ordinary run of criminal cases, but when a case of special application arises, they almost invariably muddle it.
>
> Sometimes at a late stage they ask for skilled assistance from Scotland Yard, but by then the scent is cold and, more over, a Scotland Yard detective gets very little help from the local men who regard his intrusion with great jealousy.
>
> In London we have many detectives of great experience who have, more or less, specialised in dealing with particular classes of cases. It would be a great advantage if the County Police could be induced to call in their services at an early stage, but we have no means of compelling them to do so.

Home Secretary Herbert Gladstone put the suggestion into action. London detectives, when working such cases, would involve their local counterparts in all aspects of the investigation and serve as consultants. This would minimise any feelings of jealousy or insignificance on the part of the county constabulary. Gladstone ordered that officers from the Central Office of the CID at Scotland Yard 'be specially designated for Home Office service and asked that Chief Constables should be induced to take advantage of that service in difficult cases'.

The majority of cases these officers were called to assist on would prove to be homicides. The men would soon be known as the Murder Squad. In the early twentieth century, police detection was still in its infancy. Fingerprinting was a new practice, having only been adopted by the Metropolitan Police in 1901; forensics was very much a burgeoning science. The detectives mastered their trade on the job, sharing knowledge and learning from one another. Formal training for officers up until 1905 was practically non-existent, consisting of 'two weeks on the drill square, two weeks in a police court, and an order to study an instruction manual'. By the time of the Murder Squad's creation in 1907, a training school for new police recruits had opened at Peel House in Westminster. For detectives, however, the best training to be found remained on the streets, where they cultivated contacts and learned the faces and methods of London's criminal element. The detectives of the Murder Squad brought to rural districts their big city-approach to investigating. Although the learning curve was steep, the Murder Squad was soon establishing its reputation. Its detectives became household names, their exploits printed in national newspapers.

✳

Having assumed command of Scotland Yard's famed Flying Squad a month prior, Fabian's body ached with fatigue. Established shortly after the First World War, early Flying Squad detectives hit the streets of London in powerful cars, introducing the metropolis to the thrill of high-speed police chases. The squad's detectives had spent the past several weeks tracking down members of 'a notoriously violent gang' responsible for numerous brazen robberies across London, which had netted more than £4,000 in stolen goods. As Fabian walked home in the early morning hours of 16 February 1945, he took solace in knowing the squad's first operation under his watch had met with a successful conclusion. It was past 1 a.m. by the time he reached his front door and fumbled for the keys.

Inside, the house was dark. He flicked a light switch and heard the patter of feet in another room. Fabian's bulldog, Buller, appeared in the hallway to greet his tired master. Fabian gave the dog a pat on the head and walked into the kitchen. On the counter he saw a note in his wife's handwriting: 'Telephone the CID Commander.' Thoughts of a somewhat restful morning quickly fell by the wayside. He picked up the phone and dialled the CID's number. The conversation proved mercifully brief. The Warwickshire Constabulary had requested Scotland Yard's assistance investigating the murder of an old farm labourer. Fabian listened as the commander detailed the crime. Despite his years on the force, the barbaric nature of the victim's injuries shocked Fabian. Managing only a few hours sleep, Fabian woke at 5 a.m. that morning. In the kitchen, he picked up the phone and called Whitehall 1212. When the night-duty inspector at Central Office answered, Fabian asked him to have somebody 'check the torches in one of the murder bags'. As Fabian later wrote:

> There are nine brown leather murder bags on the CID superintendent's shelf in Central Office, each of which is ready packed with every device, from rubber gloves for handling the corpse to handcuffs for pinioning the murderer. My bag also held a kind of little burglar's outfit of screwdriver, awl, nails, steel hammer, wrench, and a travelling ink-bottle, non-spillable.

The murder bag was a relatively new concept. It carried all the accoutrements an investigator in the field might need: magnifying glass, tweezers, rubber gloves, measuring tape, specimen jars, and other items vital for the processing of crime scenes. It evolved from a rather gruesome case two decades prior. In 1924, a bloodied knife and woman's clothing were discovered in a Gladstone bag in the luggage room of Waterloo Station. Patrick Mahon, the bag's owner, was arrested when he claimed his baggage. He told police that following a recent argument, he had killed his mistress in a seaside bungalow, dismembered her body, and attempted to boil her arms, legs, and other body parts to get rid of the evidence. A team of detectives immediately left London for the bungalow, situated on the Crumbles, an isolated stretch of Sussex coastline between Eastbourne and Pevesney Bay.

Entering the dwelling, detectives slapped handkerchiefs over their mouths and noses in a feign effort to block the sickening stench of decomposition. Blood evidence on the floor revealed Mahon had killed 34-year-old Evelyn Kaye, his lover, in the sitting room. Detectives followed the smeared crimson trail across the hallway, through a bedroom and into the scullery, where they found boiled body parts in a saucepan and tub. The 'heart and other internal organs' were sealed in a biscuit tin. In the sitting and dining rooms, charred bones stood out against the ashes in the fireplaces. Remnants of the woman's torso were found in a large trunk in one of the bedrooms alongside a bloodied saw. When pathologist

Bernard Spilsbury arrived at the scene to examine the remains, he was shocked to find detectives scooping up shreds of rotting flesh with their bare hands and putting it into buckets. When Spilsbury pointed out the health hazards of such an undertaking and asked a detective if he ever used rubber gloves, the detective answered no. Since the Murder Squad's formation seventeen years prior, this had been standard practice. Investigators at the time did not know the quality of evidence removed from a crime scene was directly related to how it was handled.

Spilsbury's eventual autopsy on what remained of Kaye revealed the woman had been three months pregnant. Mahon admitted to police he panicked when he learned of Kaye's pregnancy and took violent action to ensure his wife never found out. In the end, he went to the gallows. The case having run its course, Spilsbury approached Detective Superintendent William Brown, head of the Murder Squad, and shared his concerns regarding the manner in which detectives handled human remains. The end result was the murder bag. Over the years, as methods of detection and evidence gathering evolved, so too did the murder bag's contents. Some detectives, such as Fabian, personalised their bags by adding various items. One detective made sure his bag always contained a bottle of whiskey. If called out to a desolate spot in the middle of the night, it didn't hurt to bring along something to take the edge off.

Detective Sergeant Albert Webb accompanied Fabian up to the Cotswolds. The two men left London on the 9.10 a.m. train and arrived in Leamington Spa two hours later. Superintendent Alec Spooner picked them up at the station and drove them to police headquarters at Stratford-upon-Avon. There, the Yard men met with the chief constable of Warwickshire, E.R.B. Kemble, and Superintendent Simmons, who was working the investigation with Spooner. The Warwickshire officers debriefed their London counterparts on the extent of the inquiry thus far before taking them to the scene of the crime.

Fabian was a detective of high reputation when he arrived in the Cotswolds that February morning, a man of stone-cold facts and hard evidence; a seasoned investigator with an impressive track record for closing tough investigations. How hard would it be to track down a killer in leafy Warwickshire? Lower Quinton, at the time, was a village of 493 people. Someone would know something;

someone would talk – how could they not? Fabian knew he would have to tread carefully. The villagers were liable to view him with suspicion, for here was the big-city cop ready to throw his weight around. But the seemingly insular nature of country life would, perhaps, also work in his favour. London was a sprawling metropolis of countless hiding places and thousands of people minding their own business. In the city, people tend not to get involved, to look the other way in the presence of abnormality. Here, in Lower Quinton, anything out of the ordinary – strange behaviour, a small change in a daily routine – would be duly noted by the villagers. Something would surely be mentioned over the rim of a pint glass in the local pub, the College Arms. Fabian, one of Scotland Yard's great manhunters, would bring the killer to justice.

As with many English villages, time moves slowly in Lower Quinton. The village today looks much as it did back in 1945. The local pub's exterior has hardly changed in appearance and Charles Walton's house, opposite the church, looks from the outside just as it did back in the day, with its whitewashed walls and thatched roof. It was a far cry from the hustle and bustle to which Fabian was accustomed. The men got out of the car and stood in the chill winter air. Taking in the thatched roofs and the village green, the churchyard with its crooked gravestones set against rolling fields, it was hard to imagine anything violent happening in such a setting. Having now been a police officer for twenty-four years, nothing surprised Fabian much anymore. In his line of work, one grew accustomed to man's inhumanity to man. Rage, aggression, jealousy, lust, and other age-old sentiments that fuelled murder were not tempered by pretty scenery. Violence was not endemic to only the big city. Those who thought otherwise were fooling themselves. Spooner led Fabian and Webb through the churchyard in the direction of the crime scene. The killing field was approximately three quarters of a mile from Charles Walton's cottage and little more than a quarter of a mile from the nearest road running through Upper Quinton. The body, Fabian noted, was found in the extreme corner of the field, equal distance from the road at Upper Quinton to the west and Meon Lane to the east. A uniformed constable still stood guard over the spot. The ground was littered with hawthorn twigs; the grass stained with blood.

'What motive?' barked Fabian. 'Robbery, revenge, a quarrel?'

'The work of a maniac,' suggested Webb.

The ferocity of the attack pointed to something far beyond a simple robbery, an altogether unlikely motive considering Walton's habit of not carrying money. The nature of the wounds, the extent of the damage done, suggested the killer was enraged. Was it something personal? What could a frail old man, nearly crippled by rheumatism, have done to incur such wrath? The questions churned in Fabian's head as he examined the surrounding landscape. In his memoirs, Fabian incorporates legends of local witchcraft into his description of the crime scene. 'On the hilltops around Lower Quinton,' he writes, 'are circles of stones where witches are reputed to hold Sabbaths, and it was under the shadow of Meon Hill, not far from the stone circle of whispering knights, that on Valentine's Day of 1945 a rheumaticky, gnarled old man was found murdered, eight miles from Stratford-on-Avon, Warwickshire.' In the two reports he filed on the case, he makes no mention of witches or whispering knights, but the stone circle he alludes to in his book has become an integral part of the Walton murder story.

The Rollright Stones, situated on a ridge between Oxfordshire and Warwickshire, are roughly 12 miles from Lower Quinton, and not near the murder site as many accounts – including Fabian's – suggest. Three separate elements make up the Rollright Stones. Dating back as early as 2500 BC, the King's Men is a circle of seventy-seven large stones, 104 feet in diameter, built for ceremonial purposes. To the east are another five large, upright stones, the remains of a 5,000-year-old burial chamber, known as the Whispering Knights. The stones got their name 'because of the conspiratorial way in which they lay inwards towards each other, as if they are plotting against their king'. The King Stone, a single monolith worn and battered by time, stands 50 yards to the north of the King's Men. Its age and the purpose it served are not entirely known. Some speculate it was an astronomical marker; others have suggested it was a gravestone or guidepost of some kind.

Legend claims the Rollright Stones are the remains of a king 'with ambitions to conquer all of England' and his army. According to the seventeenth century antiquarian Camden, the king and his men, while out riding, encountered a local witch named Mother Shipton. The old woman played on the king's vanity, telling him,

'Seven long strides shalt thou take, and if Long Compton thou canst see, King of England thou shalt be.' The king dismounted his horse, bellowing, 'Stick, stock, stone, as King of England I shall be known.' He took seven long strides. On the final step, the ground – as if by magic – seemed to rise in front of him and obscure the view of Long Compton. The old witch cackled. 'As Long Compton thou canst not see, King of England thou shalt not be,' she intoned. 'Rise up stick and stand still stone, for King of England thou shalt be none. Thou and they men hoar stones shall be, and I myself an elder tree.'

And so the king turned to stone where he stood, thus becoming the King Stone. His army, now the King's Men, met the same fate. Four traitorous knights, who had separated from the main group and were, at that very moment, plotting against the king, could not escape the spell. They turned to stone as they quietly plotted and now remain in their conspiratorial pose as the Whispering Knights. It remains a mystery as to what the king and his men did to run afoul of the witch. Also unknown is why she turned herself into an elder tree – perhaps it was to keep eternal watch over her victims. The witch-elder grows in a row of hedges between the King Stone and the King's Men and, according to legend, 'if cut when in blossom will bleed'. Local lore claims the king and his men sometimes come to life at midnight and dance in a circle. Death or madness are supposedly the fates of anyone who stumbles upon the late-night spectacle. Other legends suggest the stones are home to faeries that live in caverns beneath the site. A story that has attached itself to the Walton murder in particular claims the stones are a place of gathering for witches. Some accounts of the Quinton murder say Walton, as a young lad, would 'steal out to the mysterious Rollright Stones nearby and watch witch rituals'.

In exaggerating the stones' location in relation to the killing field, was Fabian merely hoping to inject a little ambience into his already entertaining memoirs? Whatever the reason, the Rollright Stones, in subsequent tellings of the Walton story, have become an integral part of the crime. Now, standing over the bloodstained hawthorn twigs and matted grass in the corner of Hillground, Fabian realised the field where Walton died was not wholly isolated. A cottage sat 300 yards from the murder site. In another neighbouring field, Fabian saw a caravan and noted its occupants would have an unobstructed view of the scene. In the cottage, Spooner told Fabian, lived a Miss Feronia Gough, 33, and a 59-year-old lodger named Walter Weaver. An RAF flight lieutenant stationed at nearby Long Marston aerodrome rented the caravan with his wife. All four individuals had alibis that checked out, Spooner said. Fabian had no doubt the Warwickshire Constabulary had adequately ruled out the residents in the cottage and caravan – but, in the name of thoroughness, he would still interview them himself. In fact, he would conduct the investigation as if starting from scratch. Thus, it would be imperative to track the movements of everyone in the village on the day in question.

From where he stood, Fabian could see the thatched roofs of Lower Quinton, the steeple of St Swithin's, and the smoke of late morning fires rising from chimneys in thin wisps. It seemed a world away from the blackouts and chaos of wartime London. Surely, secrets in a village this small would be hard to keep. That's not to say Fabian didn't have his work cut out for him. There was no well-preserved crime scene. The field was a public thoroughfare; plus villagers and policemen had trampled the area the night of the murder. With so many footprints in the damp ground, it would be all but impossible to recreate what happened in Walton's final moments. The clear lack of motive also complicated matters. And what of the missing pocket watch – was there any significance in that? The victim's clothes had been disarranged and rifled through, which suggested robbery – but why murder in such a brutal fashion?

✳

Fabian and Webb established an operations room at the police station in Stratford-upon-Avon. Here, they would collate evidence, review their findings, exchange theories and, hopefully, bring the case to a rapid conclusion. On the wall, Fabian pinned a large aerial shot of Lower and Upper Quinton – and the surrounding fields – taken by a reconnaissance plane from RAF Leamington during a practice flight prior to the crime. Fabian and Webb decided they would question, personally, 'the 493 villagers of Lower Quinton, Upper Quinton, and Admington'. Based on what he learned from such interviews, Fabian would track 'with map pins, little coloured flags and threads' the comings and goings of everyone in the area that day, including Walton. Once complete, wrote Fabian, the map would 'then show where the paths crossed, murder and victim, or where the alibis proved shaky. It was the latest method from the Hendon detective school.'

Fabian's first order of business was to interview Alfred John Potter. Thus far, Walton's employer had provided nothing more than a very informal statement to Inspector Toombs of the Warwickshire Constabulary. On the afternoon of Saturday 17 February, Fabian and Webb got in their police car and drove the 8 miles from Stratford to The Firs. Potter's wife Lilian answered the knock on the door. Fabian flashed his identification and stated the purpose of his visit. Lilian seemed neither pleased nor dismayed to have the police on her doorstep. She led Fabian and Webb into the kitchen, offered them a seat at the table, and summoned her husband. Potter came in from out back. He was, Fabian saw, a man of considerable build, thick neck, broad of shoulder and a barrel chest. The farmer removed his wide-brimmed hat and shook hands with the detectives.

Dispensing of the customary pleasantries, Fabian and Webb launched into their questioning. Potter, at 40 years old, had lived at The Firs and managed the farm for the past five years. L.L. Potter & Sons, a company of which Potter's father was the proprietor, owned the farm. As Potter spoke, Lilian hovered nearby.

'What can you tell us about Walton?' asked Webb.

'I have known Charles Walton for the past five years or so,' Potter said. 'For about the past nine months I have employed him casually as a labourer on my farm. He would usually work about four days a week. He never worked in wet weather. I used to pay him eighteen pence an hour and, as a rule, I would pay him at the end of a fortnight. Sometimes I would pay him each week. I left it to him to tell me how many hours he had worked. He was an honest, hardworking old man and I always trusted him. All the winter he has been employed trimming the hedges on my farm. He would usually start at about eight o'clock in the morning, although recently it was a little later.'

'Tell us about the day of the murder,' Fabian said.

'On the morning of Wednesday, 14 February,' said Potter, rubbing his brow in thoughtful contemplation, 'at about ten past twelve, I went across to Cacks Leys, a field on my farm, to see some sheep and feed some calves. When I got there, it was about twenty past twelve and I saw Walton working at the hedge in the next field. He was about

500 yards away and working in his shirtsleeves. I am quite sure of this. This was the first occasion I had seen him in his shirtsleeves since he had been hedge cutting, and I thought to myself, "He's getting on with it today." I would have gone over to see him, but I had a heifer in a ditch nearby, which I had to attend to. I went straight back home and got there at about twenty to one. I then went to see to the heifer.'

Without prodding from the detectives, Potter detailed his grim discovery, telling how Edith had come knocking on his door that evening with Harry Beasley, and how they trudged across the fields and stumbled across Walton's savaged body. In the light of his torch, Potter said, he could see the old man's face was covered in blood. He hung about the field 'until the policeman from Long Marston arrived' and left soon thereafter.

'I had various things to attend to on my farm,' he said.

Fabian took some notes, all the while mentally summing up the man who sat across from him. Potter hardly seemed disturbed by recent events. All things considered, he presented a relatively unruffled façade. It seems odd, in the wake of his employee's murder, that Potter would say he had matters to attend to on his farm – but animals do have needs, and Fabian did not press Potter on the issue.

'Tell me about Walton,' Fabian said.

Potter replied:

All the time I have known Charles Walton, I have never had a cross word with him – and I have never known him to be in a temper. I have never heard him say a bad thing about anybody, and I don't think he had an enemy in the world. He was a man of spirit and, if attacked, I think he would have retaliated. I have never heard anyone say a thing against him, and he was respected by everybody. I have never known him to enter a public house. When he wasn't at work, he was at home. His only friend, as far as I know, was old George Higgins who lives at Lower Quinton. They used to go for walks sometimes on a Sunday.

Fabian told Webb to make note of Higgins's name and wondered just how much fight a rheumatic old man who needed two canes to get around could muster if attacked. There were no scratches or wounds of any type on Potter's face to suggest a recent altercation, nor were there any such signs of violence on his hands. If there were, the physical nature of Potter's work could have easily explained them away.

'Did you see anyone else in the fields that day?' from Webb.

Potter shook his head.

'I saw nobody about the part of the farm where Walton was working,' he said. 'It is not unusual to see soldiers, airmen, and Italian prisoners walking across the fields of my farm, but I did not see any that day.'

A mere 2 miles from the crime scene was the Italian Prisoner of War camp in Long Marston, home to 1,043 inmates. From London, Scotland Yard was dispatching a fluent Italian speaker to handle the prisoner interviews.

'You're certain,' Fabian said, 'that it was Walton you saw working the hedge that afternoon?'

Potter said:

Although I cannot be positive, I am almost certain it was Walton who I saw working at twenty past twelve. Whoever it was appeared to be trimming the hedge. From the point where I saw Walton to where he had finished working was about 10 yards. It would have taken him about half an hour to have trimmed that amount of hedge.

Potter said Walton would have been done with the hedge in about a week. The Yard detectives thanked Potter for his time and got up to leave. Potter walked them to the door and bid them a good afternoon. After two decades in law enforcement, Fabian knew how to read people, but it was too soon to form an opinion of Potter. He needed more information. In order to find out what happened to Walton, he would have to uncover the hidden story around the killing, unravel the events of the day and put them in their proper place. To that end, he needed to establish motive and reconstruct the events in the field. Fabian and Webb returned to the police station in Stratford-upon-Avon and began working the phones. By early afternoon, officers from the Warwickshire Constabulary were back in the field en force, canvassing the area for any shred of evidence. Alfred James Hinksman, Warwickshire police sergeant No. 165, was one of the men out there that winter's afternoon. Along the upper edge of a bean field neighbouring the field in which Walton died, Hinksman found a line of footprints 'made by a boot with round studs and steel tips and heel plates, similar to Army boots'. The prints extended the entire upper length of the bean field, crossed into Hillground, and made their way down the side farthest from where Walton fell. They stopped at a point where the individual clambered over a bush and continued in the neighbouring field toward Upper Quinton. The prints were not of a sufficient quality for casts to be made.

Continuing his search, Hinksman found another set of prints made by a similar boot, 'leading up the side of the bean field from the scene of the crime towards Meon Hill'. Hinksman followed the prints to the top of the field, where it was clearly evident the boots' owner had climbed over a fence that ran along the field's northern edge. The prints continued through a ploughed field on the other side of the fence and disappeared into the woods on Meon Hill. The last of the footprints were just beyond the woods' treeline. 'After that,' Hinksman noted in his report, 'all trace of the footprints was lost.' The prints leading into the wood were defined well enough to warrant the making of a cast, although it was impossible to say when the prints had been made. Detective Sergeant Medley, summoned by Hinksman, knelt over one of the prints and carefully filled it with plaster.

No one could say with any certainty whether the footprint belonged to the killer, but the cast could be used to help reinforce a charge of murder in the event a suspect was arrested. The searching of the field and surrounding countryside continued for several days. 'We had brought the 20th century to Lower Quinton like a cold shower-bath,' Fabian later wrote. Through the intervention of his superiors in London, calls were placed to the Ministry of Defence, requesting a reconnaissance plane stationed at RAF Leamington fly over the crime scene and take pictures. Soldiers from the Royal Engineers, 407 Company, were dispatched to Hillground to sweep the area with their metal detectors and search for Walton's missing pocket watch. With any luck, it would be found with the killer's fingerprints on it. 'I have considered,' Fabian wrote in a case report, 'the possibility of [the watch] having either been thrown away by the murderer in the nearby fields or it having fallen from his clothing when the body was carried across the fields to the ambulance.'

When the aerial photograph taken by the reconnaissance plane was developed and delivered to Fabian at the Stratford-upon-Avon

Police Station, the level of detail stunned him. It 'showed even the bloodstains, the trodden grass around the murder scene – and every twig for a full mile in all directions'. This became the map by which he would now track the movements of the villagers that day.

While the canvassing of the fields continued, Fabian and Webb set out to piece together Walton's final morning. They spoke with Edith, who, although still shaken, ran them through her uncle's daily routine. Still leaning towards robbery as a possible motive, Fabian asked Edith about her uncle's finances. He made little and never carried money around, she said. What about insurance? Fabian asked. 'My uncle was not insured,' Edith said. 'He had an account with the Midland Bank, Stratford-upon-Avon, but I don't know how much he had in it. My uncle left a will in which I believe I receive nearly everything.'

Perhaps, thought Fabian, the bank account might reveal something.

Outside Walton's thatched cottage, the church steeple stood in contrast against a cloudy sky. The two detectives cut through the churchyard and into the neighbouring field before reaching the caravan Fabian had noticed while examining the murder scene. Officers from the Warwickshire Constabulary had already interviewed the occupants, Thomas Arthur Woodward and his wife, Dorothy, but Fabian wanted to hear for himself what they had to say. The airman invited Fabian and Webb into the cramped confines of his home. The couple told the detectives they had been living in the caravan since November 1944. Thomas, a flight lieutenant, was stationed at the aerodrome in Long Marston.

Thomas said:

I knew Charles Walton by sight, as he passed my caravan daily to and from work. On the morning of 14 February, I was standing at the door of my caravan at about 8.15 a.m., when I saw the old chap come through the churchyard gate towards me. He walked past the caravan and through the fields in the direction of Meon Hill. I remember the time very well, as I was being picked up that morning at 8.30 a.m. by an RAF van at the church. I arrived back at the van at approximately 5.30 that night. As I was sitting at tea a short time after, I was approached by a woman who I understand was Mr Walton's niece and a man, Mr Beasley. They asked me if I could direct them to the field where he was working and said they were worried because he had not arrived home. I didn't know where the old chap was working, but my wife pointed out to them the direction in which he generally went. The following morning I was told by Mr Potter, our landlord, that the old chap had been killed. That was the first I knew anything about it.

Dorothy, sitting next to her husband with a baby in her arms, also said she knew the old man by sight. She saw him walk past the caravan at roughly 8.10 a.m. on the morning of 14 February. The field in which he'd been working was about a quarter mile away from the caravan.

'Our windows overlook the fields of Firs Farm,' she said, pointing to the view. 'I can actually see the field where Mr Walton's body was found. The stile near where the body was found is visible from the windows.'

From where he sat, Fabian could see the stile in the near distance.

'Did you see anyone, other than Walton, that morning?'

'No,' Dorothy replied:

I didn't leave the caravan that day. As far as I can remember, I didn't see anyone until about six o'clock when Miss Walton and Mr Beasley called to ask me if I knew where the old man had been working. The following morning, I heard Mr Walton's body had been found.

'You didn't see Mr Potter about?' Fabian asked.

'I didn't see Mr Potter or any farm hands.'

'What about Italians from the nearby prison camp,' asked Webb, 'do you ever see them wandering about?'

'I've never seen any Italians near the field where Mr Walton was killed,' she said, 'but one or two of them have been in the field where my caravan is.'

The detectives left the caravan and crossed the fields, heading in the direction of the murder scene. In his statement, Potter said he had visited the field adjacent to the one in which Walton had been working that fateful morning. Doing so would have taken him right past the caravan. Mrs Woodward, however, said she saw no one pass her home. Of course, if she had been tending to a crying baby, she would have most likely been oblivious to anyone walking by. Fabian now wanted to talk with the residents of the cottage that stood only 300 yards from where Walton died. It was a house of grey stone with an almost perfect view of the murder site, save a row of hedges that partially obscured the scene.

Feronia Gough, who rented the cottage, told Fabian and Webb she worked cleaning houses in the neighbouring villages. On the day Walton died, she left home early in the morning for a job in Upper Quinton. At about noon, she paid a visit to her aunt's house and picked up some meat to prepare dinner for herself and fellow lodger Walter Weaver, who worked as a print setter with Edith at the Royal Society of Arts. Weaver, also home and available to answer Fabian's questions, said he returned from work for his midday meal on 14 February at one o'clock and remained chatting with Miss Gough until the two left the house together roughly an hour later. Weaver returned to work, and Gough went to meet a friend for the afternoon in Stratford-upon-Avon. Neither one of them saw anyone in the field where Walton was working, nor, while home for lunch, did either one hear the sounds of any sort of altercation in the nearby field. Fabian jotted down the names of Gough's aunt, cleaning clients, and the friend she met the day of the murder. Her statement would have to be checked – as would Weaver's – but he knew already they would pan out. There was nothing untoward about either of them. Gough was a slight woman in her early 30s and hardly someone Fabian considered capable of such brutality. Weaver was an elderly gentleman of quiet disposition. Nothing about his physicality or demeanour suggested he possessed the rage or wherewithal to murder. Besides, what possible motive would either one have? 'There is no reason to believe,' Fabian wrote, 'that they [are] connected in any way with the death of Charles Walton.'

Outside, Fabian and Webb crossed to the other side of the hedgerow that ran past the cottage and entered the field where Walton had been working that day. There was no longer a constable standing over the scene, but dark stains were still evident in the grass, marking the spot where Walton fell. Not for the first time, Fabian was struck by the silence of the place. The city was Fabian's normal hunting ground with all the noise and chaos that entailed. One would expect people to claim not to have seen or heard anything out of the ordinary. Fabian had no doubt the people he had spoken to thus far were telling the truth, but he found it hard to believe that nothing in the easily disturbed ecosystem of small village life seemed even slightly askew on the day Walton died. Of course, it was still early in the investigation. But here, they were outsiders – strangers prying into everyone's business. Who was to say anyone would talk, even if they did know something? Being suspicious of people was part of being a cop.

Back in the village, Fabian and Webb followed the only option available to them. They knocked on doors and questioned anyone who passed them in the narrow streets. Surely, sooner or later, they would come across someone who had seen something. Their inquiries brought them into contact with two more residents who saw Walton walking into the fields on the morning of 14 February. At 19 Lower Quinton, just four doors down from Walton's home, the detectives questioned 73-year-old Joseph Waters. Crippled with a bad leg, Waters was sitting on his front doorstep on the morning in question and saw Walton pass through the churchyard at about 9.30 a.m. He spent the remainder of the day in his house and didn't see anyone else. At nearby Manor House, the front windows of which offered an unobstructed view of the churchyard, the detectives spoke with Charlotte Byway, a 73-year-old spinster who worked as a children's nurse for the house's owner.

'At 9 a.m. I was upstairs when I noticed Charles Walton, who was known to me by sight, enter the churchyard from the road,' she said:

He had a sack over his shoulder, but it didn't look to have anything in it. He was walking with two sticks – one an ordinary short walking stick and the other a long stick, as tall or taller than himself. I didn't notice which way he went after entering the churchyard. I came downstairs just afterwards and didn't see anyone else about.

The detectives now had four witnesses who had seen Walton walk through the churchyard on his way to work. Fabian dismissed the discrepancies in time as honest mistakes on the part of each witness. What the statements proved was that Walton walked to work alone and did not appear to have been followed by anyone.

✳

Back at the operations room in the Stratford-upon-Avon Police Station, Fabian found a copy of the *Stratford-upon-Avon Herald* lying on his desk. Dated that day, 16 February, the lead on the front page was headlined:

OLD MAN'S TERRIBLE INJURIES
Inflicted with Billhook and Pitchfork
TRAGIC DISCOVERY AT QUINTON

Warwickshire police are investigating what may prove to be a murder of particularly brutal character. On Wednesday night, following a search, the body of a 74-year-old farm labourer, Charles Walton of Lower Quinton, was found with terrible injuries at Meon Hill where he had engaged in hedge-laying. A trouncing hook and two-tined pitchfork are said to have been embedded in his body.

Mr Walton, who lived with his niece, was a frail old man. He suffered considerably with rheumatism and walked with the aid of two sticks.

However, he still did odd jobs for local farmers, and on Wednesday morning set off to work at the Hill grounds, a lonely spot about a mile from his home ...

Maybe the article would prompt someone, somewhere, to come forward.

4

FABIAN OF THE YARD

In early 1926, Fabian passed his first detective's exam and made the rank of detective constable – this, however, did not mean major cases were quick to come his way. Fabian was still very much a junior officer. He spent many shifts trolling the lobbies of London's hotels and the dark, smoke-filled crypts of West End clubs, looking for crime. He would eventually become one of the Met's foremost experts on London's club land, helping co-author Scotland Yard's 'The Club Book', a thick, black tome listing the more than 300 registered and off-the-book establishments within a one-mile radius of Piccadilly Circus.

The Union Club was an underground haunt for French gangsters at 24 Frith Street. To access its smoky interior, one entered a door at street level and walked down a cramped hallway that led to a wooden flight of stairs, which, in turn, descended to a door layered in thick, green baize and studded with bolts. Beyond the door, another flight of stairs dropped to another entryway, which opened onto the actual club. The establishment was not a place one would deem high class. A wooden bar stretched the length of the room on one side. The other furnishings consisted of a few billiard tables, two flashing fruit machines, and a few tables and chairs. Murals of a sexual nature covered the walls. A red-brick fireplace dominated one corner of the room. Beside the ash-filled hearth, a man lay dead on the floor. Fabian stood over the corpse, viewing a body for the first time. More importantly, he was working his first murder case.

Luck of the draw had brought him to the underground confines of the Union Club. It was 5 April 1926, Easter Monday, and the senior Vice Squad officers at Vine Street were home with their families. Being the junior-ranking officer – and having just made detective several months prior – Fabian pulled holiday duty. The CID office was deserted that evening; the phones silent. With nothing better to do, Fabian had planned to spend the night reading his textbooks and studying for his next police exam. The jangling phone nearly startled him out of his chair. He fumbled for the earpiece. It was the duty inspector calling to say a shooting had been reported in Soho at the Union Club. Fabian knew the place well. It was the same place he had observed the French gangsters several months prior. He hung up the phone, his pulse pounding. He grabbed his hat and darted for the door. Arriving at the club within minutes, he worked his way through the crowd of gawkers gathered at the street-level entrance. He nodded at the uniformed constable standing guard and descended, literally, into London's underworld.

The club's stunned clientele stood in silence around the edge of the room, staring at the body. A shapely blonde in a form-fitting black dress sat weeping on a bar stool. Fabian knelt beside the victim, who lay sprawled on his back. There was no mystery regarding the cause of death, as a bloody bullet hole in the victim's abdomen was clearly evident. Fabian stood up and looked about the place. Broken billiard cues littered a floor cluttered with overturned tables, broken chairs, and the jagged remains of bottles and glasses. Then there was the smell, a sickening composite of alcohol, sweat, and gunpowder. The two-dozen or so club regulars – accustomed to seeing Fabian as a harmless entity, sipping water at the bar – now looked upon him with a sudden air of suspicion. 'They were bad characters, and they all stared at me,' Fabian later wrote. 'I knew some of the people there, and I could see some of them knew me, too, and no mistake this time – a detective!' Fabian turned to a police sergeant and ordered that no one be allowed to leave.

When the sergeant saluted and addressed Fabian as 'sir', the young detective constable felt the blood rush to his face. So, this is what it was like to head an investigation! Fabian moved to a phone behind the bar and called Scotland Yard Headquarters to request a photographer and fingerprint technician.

Fabian could feel the weight of angry stares as he hung up the phone. He addressed the crowded room in a stern voice, doing his utmost to convey authority and assert his control.

'What happened?' he barked. 'Who is he – and who did it?'

At first, no one answered. The attention of the club goers seemed to shift from Fabian to random spots on the ceiling. One man busied himself dabbing blood from a split lip, but eventually the story emerged in random fragments of French. Fabian knew they all spoke English but were now addressing him in their native tongue just to make matters difficult. It hardly mattered. During his time in the Soho clubs, Fabian had picked up enough rudimentary French to get by. The victim was a Parisian named Baladda, visiting London on holiday. At some point in the evening, he teased a man at one of the billiard tables. The target of Baladda's jest drew a pistol without warning and shot Baladda dead. Did anyone, Fabian asked, know the killer or try to stop him? A smarmy-looking man with gold teeth stepped forward.

'Yes, policeman,' he said with obvious contempt. 'I hit him with a billiard cue. I broke his scalp – but he escaped.'

The crowd murmured its consent. As Fabian pondered his next move, he made eye contact with the billiard-marker standing in a corner of the room. The man winked and flashed Fabian a knowing grin. Realising the man had something to say – but couldn't say it here without putting his life in danger – Fabian made a show of singling out the billiard-marker and hauling him off to the police station. The onlookers voiced their disapproval as Fabian seemed to be harassing one of their own without cause. The billiard-marker played his part, protesting as Fabian escorted him from the premises. At the Vine Street Police Station, however, he seemed to have second thoughts about cooperating. Suddenly, he knew nothing – but Fabian was persistent. His incessant questioning slowly eroded the man's resistance. The witness at last blurted out the victim's first name: Charles. And what, Fabian wanted to know, did this Charles Baladda do for a living? The billiard-marker wiped sweat from his glistening upper lip, knowing the answer would reveal much about the dead man.

'He was an acrobat.'

Fabian leaned back in his chair and allowed himself a smile. 'Charles the Acrobat' was a French gangster of notorious repute. In fact, he had been the target of Fabian's surveillance only several weeks prior at the Union Club, the night French girls dubbed Fabian 'The Little Water Drinker'. That same night, a rival French gangster – Emile Berthier, alias 'Mad Emile' – had shown up at the club with several of his henchmen. Although both sides played nice, the atmosphere had been, in Fabian's words, 'as prickly as a hairbrush'. Fabian now asked the billiard-marker who pulled the trigger – but he already knew the answer. The witness confirmed Mad Emile had indeed fired the fatal shot, the result of some feud that commenced months earlier in Paris. As Fabian pondered this information, a booming voice behind him demanded to know the status of the investigation.

Fabian turned to see the Vine Street divisional inspector, accompanied by the district superintendent, entering the room. A small army of uniformed and plainclothes officers followed close behind. The young detective constable, believing this to be his moment to shine, informed the newcomers they had a gangland killing on their hands. He named the victim and the suspect, expecting to be congratulated for his work so far. What he got instead was a hard lesson in police work. Had Fabian, the divisional inspector wanted to know, checked with area doctors, hospitals, and chemists to see if Berthier had sought treatment for his head wound? Had he dispatched men to the train stations in the event Berthier – at this very moment – was trying to leave town? Had he retrieved the man's photograph for circulation from the Aliens Office? Had he checked the suspect's background with the Criminal Records Office? Fabian could do nothing more than bluster through his answers. With so many experienced officers in the room, he suddenly felt very inadequate. The divisional inspector frowned at Fabian's amateur performance and told him he would have to do better if he expected to make it as a detective.

He now turned to the other officers and began belting orders. Within minutes, detectives were hitting the streets, heading to hospitals to review recent admissions; tracking down informants to ply them for any information they may have; to question those still at the Union Club; and to canvas railway stations. Not until Fabian was the last man in the room did the divisional inspector issue him orders. He was to head immediately to St George's Hospital, before checking out Victoria Station, Westminster Hospital, and – finally – Waterloo Station.

Fabian later remembered:

In an instant, I had fallen from my smug position of Sherlock Holmes in charge of the Baladda murder. I was just another of the team of detectives combing London for the injured Mad Emile. The superintendent was absolutely right. Crimes are solved by good teamwork, not prima donnas. It was a lesson I never forgot.

Fabian, accompanied by a sergeant, checked the hospitals, all to no avail, before making his way to Victoria Station, the second busiest railway terminus in Britain after Waterloo. Inside, beneath the great skylights and latticed ironwork, the station thrummed with organised chaos. Fabian eyed the bustling masses and quickly realised he was searching for the proverbial needle. He began scouring the platforms, trying to scan every face in the crowd. He positioned himself near the doors of soon-to-be departing trains and carefully watched the passengers boarding. Nothing. He and the sergeant next canvassed the waiting rooms, suspicious of anyone hiding behind a newspaper. Again, their efforts proved futile. At the continental booking office, the ticket agent said no one with a head wound had recently booked passage on any train. Perhaps, Fabian thought, his suspect would be in need of a drink to calm the nerves and numb the pain of the injury, but a check of the bars turned up nothing. In one of the station's washrooms, Fabian's luck changed. The attendant reported seeing a man – someone he believed to be a foreigner – nursing a head wound, dabbing a bloody gash with a handkerchief. The man had asked the attendant when the next train to Newhaven was leaving. The attendant, accustomed to merely handing patrons towels to dry their hands and face, was shocked someone had asked him such a question.

Fabian phoned the police station and reported his findings. Scotland Yard's Special Branch was immediately notified and dispatched officers to Newhaven to pick up the hunt. Fabian, meanwhile, was ordered to return to the Union Club. As he made his way back to Frith Street, he couldn't help but wonder how long this night would drag on. Winnie, whom he had married the previous year and settled into a house in Harvest Road, Kilburn, was home alone and nine months pregnant with their first child. Thankfully, the Vine

Street duty sergeant had called her to say Fabian would be late. The district superintendent was at the crime scene when Fabian finally arrived and, in a gruff manner, chastised him for taking too long. Only later did Fabian realise this gentle ribbing was the superintendent's way of expressing satisfaction with a job well done. Fabian and a detective named Symes were left to guard the club – and the dead body that still lay by the lifeless fireplace. As the hours ticked away into the night, the place took on a discomforting atmosphere. The only illumination came courtesy of two dim bulbs 'under scarlet lampshades'. Fabian couldn't help but stare at the corpse in the corner. The late hour and the unnatural silence began to play on his imagination. He suddenly became aware of a gentle, rhythmic beating sound and wondered if the dead man's heart was pumping blood again. A quick investigation revealed it was merely the ticking of the victim's pocket watch amplified against the club's cold floor.

For a young man with a pregnant wife at home ready to deliver at any moment, the waiting seemed interminable. Part of him was desperate to simply up and leave, but he knew that to be an impossibility. Whining about the circumstances was also out of the question. A police officer, he had been taught, never complains while on the job. Not until 9 a.m. the following morning did the coroner, accompanied by two French coroners, show up to remove the body. Fabian leapt from his chair and told Symes he was heading home. Symes, a senior officer, gently reminded Fabian he couldn't do that until he had filled out his duty diary and filed an expense report for the cab he'd taken the night before to and from Victoria Station, and the late-night sandwiches he had purchased.

'What about overtime?' Fabian inquired.

Symes smirked. 'They've never heard of that word at Scotland Yard.'

When a bleary-eyed Fabian returned to Vine Street to complete the required paperwork, the superintendent summoned him to his office. Detectives from Special Branch had seized Mad Emile on a boat leaving Newhaven. Fabian had taken down his first murderer. The news made him giddy with excitement. The stress of the previous night's efforts – and the embarrassment of being dressed down in front of other officers – now seemed worth it. At his desk, he phoned Winnie at home to share the news. Winnie, sounding tired but happy, told Fabian to come home so he could tell his newborn son.

✳

Fabian continued his policing education. By 1929, he had worked a wide variety of cases, including two homicides and a major forgery investigation. On 3 July, he began an eighteen-month posting in the Criminal Records Office. Although Fabian considered the CRO assignment boring with little prospect for action, it proved beneficial to his understanding of criminals. As one Scotland Yard historian notes, 'In answering the ever-ringing telephones and also indexing cards, he learnt the way that criminals' minds worked, their *modus operandi*, how their traits, quirks, habits and peculiarities were recorded and how one could make an input into the system and make use of it.'

In February 1931, he was promoted to 'detective sergeant (second class)' and posted to Marylebone Lane, D-Division. He would continue to build his reputation, working one successful case after another. In the first week of September 1932, a gunman made criminal history when he became the first armed robber to hold-up a West End jewellery store 'in broad daylight and walk away unscathed with a fortune in his pocket'. The thief had worked quickly, drawing his gun as he entered the store and forcing the three employees into a storage room in the back. He then loaded his pockets and made his getaway, leaving no fingerprints or any other discernible clue. As the culprit fled down Oxford Street, he passed a beggar in search of a handout. The thief spat invective at the man, cursing at him in a foreign language. The beggar recoiled in surprise and watched the man disappear into the street's bustling crowd of shoppers, which never seems to dissipate.

When Fabian arrived on the scene later that day, he put his knowledge of London to work. In a place as crowded as Oxford Street, someone must have seen something. Fabian knew the street to be a favourite working spot for 'gutter musicians, beggars, [and] kerb salesmen'. Two days of searching and asking questions turned up the beggar reproached by the armed robber. The man told Fabian he saw the suspect peering through the jewellery shop window before entering and then fleeing the premises several minutes later. The thief did not run, but walked away quickly. He cussed in Arabic, the beggar said. Fabian, surprised, asked the beggar how he knew it was Arabic. The beggar smiled and said he knew how to swear in many languages. Fabian now began canvassing pawnshops with a list and description of the stolen goods, which included a gold cigarette case engraved with a map of the world. One pawnbroker, when shown the list, told Fabian he'd heard talk in a local pub of a man trying to sell such a case. At the pub, the barman told Fabian the man in question was no regular and had only been in once. The customer had told the barman he had acquired the case overseas while recently serving with the Palestine Police. It was the lead Fabian needed.

At the London headquarters of the Palestine Police, he learned the names of men recently discharged. One of them, a Londoner named Rudolph Franklyn, matched descriptions given by the bartender and the beggar. Franklyn's final paycheque had recently been mailed to him via registered post, but the Palestine Police clerk had kept no record of Franklyn's address. Fortunately, the post office from which the cheque had been sent had a carbon copy of the mailing receipt with the man's Gloucester Road address. On 4 October 1932, Fabian – with a detective-officer as back-up – took Franklyn into custody. In the man's bedroom, under his pillow, Fabian found a snub-nosed automatic pistol equipped with a silencer. Up on a charge of robbery at the Old Bailey, Franklyn said he stole because he was out of work and too proud to beg. He received a sentence of three years and twenty lashes.

'Like most jobs,' Fabian later wrote:

detective work calls for its own special qualities of character, not the least of which is the possession of a scavenging mind. Wherever a detective goes there are tit-bits of knowledge – snatches of foreign language, odd facts about company law, medicine, local customs, travel, toxicology, or what have you – which may at some future date prove of decisive value in unravelling a baffling case. He must be prepared to mix on equal terms with a duke or a dustman, a bishop or a pickpocket – in short, to be as versatile as any quick-change actor. He must be tactful, courageous, painstaking, vigilant … let me just add that he should be a wizard at jigsaws – and leave it at that.

To solve a jigsaw puzzle, of course, one needs all the pieces.

✴

On the evening of 12 February 1939, a man named John Roman entered the Vine Street Police Station and said he needed to speak with a detective. The desk sergeant summoned Fabian. Roman told Fabian he had just gone to visit a friend in her Dover Street apartment, only to find her dead. Frightened, he touched nothing and came immediately to the police station. The victim was a prostitute named Georgina Hoffman, known in certain circles as 'The Black Butterfly'. She earned her sobriquet, the newspapers would soon report, because 'she was a fluttering, black-haired beauty'.

Fabian – along with his superior officer Detective-Superintendent Peter Beveridge – arrived on the scene at 10.30 p.m. The flat, although ransacked, was tastefully decorated with cream-coloured walls and matching furniture. Hoffman's body lay just inside the front door. The dead woman was nude with the exception of her blood-soaked underslip pushed around her neck. She lay on her back with her head pointing towards the door. She had been stabbed near her left breast and was bleeding from the nose and mouth. Beveridge and Fabian knelt beside the body and noticed the woman had false teeth, several of which were broken. Blood from a stab wound to her upper back pooled beneath her neck and shoulders. Throughout the small flat, the carpet was heavily stained with blood – as were the sheets on the bed, which was situated to the right of the flat's front door. Although the bed did not appear to have been slept in, the bolster, wet with blood, lay at the head of the mattress.

Fabian and Beveridge moved slowly through the flat. Behind the front door, Fabian found 'blood smears, which would appear to have been caused by the deceased woman's hair and the body being dragged along the floor to where it was found'. Near where the smeared trail of blood began was a lady's white blouse, which bore a knife-shaped crimson stain. Alongside the blouse was a blood-soaked bra, its shoulder straps sliced by a sharp blade. On the bed sheets, the detectives found a woman's undervest, which had been sliced up the front. Other items of women's clothing – all showing signs of having been ripped from the woman's body – were found under the bed's bloody eiderdown. As the detectives continued their search, they found additional proof of the assailant's brutality: three broken artificial teeth knocked from the woman's mouth. One was found among the bed sheets; the other two on the floor on either side of the bed. 'The Black Butterfly's ornaments, small toys, decorated the mantelshelf near my elbow – a rabbit with big ears, a woolly Scottie, a Dresden china figure,' Fabian later wrote. 'I regarded them blankly, but they gave me no hint, no light – yet somewhere in that room there must be, I felt, the first thread of a clue.'

There was a certain innocence to the woman's choice of trinkets, one at odds with what the detectives found in a drawer in the dressing table: a book of 'indecent photographs and a box of rubber sheaths'. In the wardrobe, Beveridge discovered a vast array of lingerie, including 'one pair of flagellation corsets and one pair of flagellation gloves'. Fabian looked once more at the woman, her long, midnight-coloured hair matted with blood. Detective Sergeant Percy Law from the Photograph Branch arrived at the flat shortly before midnight and took pictures of the scene. The death of an attractive woman, always a magnet for headlines, quickly earned Hoffman's murder a prominent place on the front page of London's newspapers. Crime reporters, tapping their police contacts, spilled considerable ink on the case. 'Black Butterfly is Slashed to Death in London,' headlines announced on 13 February, the morning after the body was discovered. Reported the Associated Press in an article that ran on both sides of the Atlantic:

> The stiletto slaying of a comely Irish girl known as 'The Black Butterfly' in her fashionable London apartment gave Scotland Yard a clue today in an effort to run down a 'ring' behind a series of bombings attributed to the outlawed, king-hating Irish Republican Army.

Although Fabian would, in due time, find himself in the midst of an IRA bomb plot, the newspapers overplayed the terrorist angle in the Georgina Hoffman murder. Indeed, Fabian and Beveridge wrapped the case up rather quickly. Talking to the woman's landlord, the detectives learned Georgina had rented the flat no more than two weeks prior. She had told the landlord she needed a place to stay while visiting from Glasgow. The landlord, wise to the fact Georgina was a prostitute, nevertheless rented her the place. The landlord said he knocked on Hoffman's door two days prior, on the evening of 10 February, to collect the rent. He spoke to a man with a speech impediment who said Hoffman had stepped out for a while. Believing the man was a friend of the victim's, the landlord said he would try again later.

Roman, who found the body, told Fabian and Beveridge he had seen Hoffman in the company of a man with a speech impediment over the past several days. The victim's sister, also a prostitute, said the same thing when questioned later that night. Roman and the sister were taken to the Vine Street Police Station to flip through mug shots. The woman spent a considerable amount of time turning the pages of the thick book, until she stopped and pointed with a trembling figure at one image in particular. The mug shot was that of 23-year-old Arthur James Mahoney, who had a prior conviction for stabbing a former girlfriend. Early the next morning, 13 February, detectives knocked on the door of Mahoney's house in Brixton. He seemed to be expecting the police and invited them in. Upstairs, he said, they would find the bloody knife.

When questioned at Vine Street, Mahoney said he had first seen Georgina in Piccadilly Circus and approached her. He spent several days in her company, giving her money and buying her necessities, such as cigarettes. On the night of 12 February, it became apparent to Mahoney he was simply being used for what little money he had. He confronted Georgina in her flat, the fight escalating with each word that passed between them until his temper got the better of him. In court, Mahoney escaped the hangman but would spend the rest of his life in Broadmoor Lunatic Asylum. Because of Mahoney's lineage, the press continued to report the Hoffman murder was somehow linked to the IRA, which had launched a terrorist campaign against London during 'The Black Butterfly' investigation. The timing of the attacks was purely coincidental but would soon thrust Fabian into the national spotlight.

On 15 January, the IRA had essentially declared war on Britain, after Foreign Secretary Lord Halifax ignored a demand from the group to withdraw all British forces from Ireland. The following day, five bombs went off in London, damaging several power stations. Two explosions of a more severe nature rocked the London Underground at the Tottenham Court Road and Leicester Square stations on 4 February. The timed explosives were placed in suitcases and left in the luggage rooms of both stations overnight. The bombs caused extensive damage, but – fortunately – injured only two people. The attacks continued throughout the country on an almost daily basis. On 10 June, explosions ripped through thirty post offices and mailboxes in London, Birmingham, and Manchester, with seventeen bombs having been detonated within a two-hour period.

On the evening of 24 June, Fabian was sitting at his desk in the Vine Street Police Station, banging out a report on what he believed to be one of Scotland Yard's 'wobbliest typewriters,' when a bomb detonated at the nearby intersection of Glasshouse Street and Piccadilly. The blast's concussion rattled the precinct windows and scattered the papers on his desk. He leapt from his chair, grabbed his gas mask from a nearby coat hook, and ran towards the commotion. The neon advertising signs that usually saturated Piccadilly Circus in a Technicolor dazzle had gone dark. Broken glass, shredded cigars, shattered stonework, and other random bits of debris – scattered by a bomb that only moments before had obliterated a tobacconist's – crunched beneath the detective's feet at the devastated street corner. Where the tobacco store window, with its display of humidors, pipes, and lighters had once been, there was now a smouldering void. Flames flickered around the edges. The broken glass on the pavement reflected the light in shades of red and orange, lending a kaleido-scopic quality to the scene. Silk lingerie from a neighbouring store 'shimmered in crumpled little pools' of assorted colours. The blast's concussion had shattered the windows of nearby Westminster Bank and a Chinese restaurant across the street, and hurled a newspaper seller down the steps of the Piccadilly Circus Underground Station. Traffic was brought to an immediate standstill and quickly diverted to allow fire engines to get to the scene. Witnesses told police 'that two men drove up in a taxi, that one of them threw something, and that the other disappeared in the crowd'. One man, seen running from the scene, was nearly lynched by an angry crowd before being rescued by a number of constables and taken to the Vine Street Police Station for questioning.*

Breathless, Fabian assessed the damage and noticed a package near the traffic signal. Behind him a sizeable crowd had gathered, kept at bay by several Bobbies who cast the occasional nervous glance in Fabian's direction. The package looked not unlike a shipping parcel,

---

* He was later released and not charged with any crime.

a box secured by two thick strips of black adhesive tape. Had the explosion blown it from the store? Doubtful, thought Fabian, slowly reaching out to touch the box. He quickly pulled back his hand, surprised by the heat radiating from the package.

'Keep the crowds back,' Fabian shouted to a nearby constable. 'I think there's another bomb!'

Fabian mopped his forehead with the back of his hand and knelt beside the ominous parcel. He pulled a penknife from his coat pocket, slowly worked the blade through the tape, and unwrapped one end of the parcel. He slipped his hand inside the paper and pulled out 'something that felt like a sausage wrapped in greased paper'. For a moment, Fabian believed he had merely stumbled upon someone's discarded lunch. He pictured the gathered crowd laughing, pointing fingers as he handled nothing more threatening than a few pork links. It would take years to live that sort of embarrassment down. He shrugged the thought aside, ignoring the sweat burning his eyes and the sickening stench of cordite. Wrapped in the paper were yellow tubes of soft, greasy gelignite, an explosive composite made of nitroglycerin, potassium nitrate, and wood pulp. One-by-one, Fabian placed the 4 ounce sticks – ten in total – on the littered pavement. A fuse protruded from one of the tubes. Fabian sliced the putty-like material with his knife, not knowing 'that a knife-blade can explode gelignite if it rasps upon the grit in it,' removed the fuse, and stuck it in his pocket.

Looking behind him to see how the constables were handling the crowd, Fabian was surprised to find a West End pickpocket named Charlie – a thief of some repute – had snuck under the police cordon and, employing skills necessary for his particular trade, crept up on Fabian unnoticed. Charlie was crouched low, hands on knees, and peering over Fabian's shoulder. Cordial and totally unfazed by the circumstances, Charlie asked in his thick cockney accent if there was anything he could do to help. Fabian, his hands sticky from the putty-like explosives, thanked Charlie for the kind offer but told him to get lost. If he blew himself sky high, that was one thing – but he had no intention of taking someone else with him. Slowly, Fabian sliced into more gelignite and cut the tubes into small pieces. With the help of several other brave officers, Fabian collected some cigar boxes from the storefront's shattered window and placed a piece of gelignite in each box. The boxes were taken back to the Vine Street Police Station and submerged in one of the red metal fire buckets.

On the night of Fabian's heroic act, another six bombs – including another two in Piccadilly Circus – went off in the capital and injured twenty people, including a 17-year-old boy who was permanently blinded. Even before the first bombs had gone off, Scotland Yard had been working to identify IRA extremists in London. 'The New IRA men used to hang around the lodging-houses of Leinster Gardens and have their occasional drink in their favourite houses,' Fabian later wrote. 'Most were young, had never left home before, were home-sick, and sought the Irish districts of London.' Special Branch, in the meantime, had been looking into whether gelignite had been reported stolen anywhere in the country in recent months. It transpired large quantities of the stuff had been taken from several Midland quarries. Detectives, working their informants, learned 60 pounds of gelignite had been 'smuggled by truck' to two addresses in London's Irish district prior to the Piccadilly bombings. The addresses in question were lodging houses the Yard knew were occupied by IRA 'fanatics'.

It fell on Fabian to raid the premises and make arrests. Fabian was told he and his men could arm themselves for the operation if they wished. It was known the occupants in the building were well armed. After giving the matter some thought, Fabian decided against the use of revolvers. The IRA, he reasoned, was politically motivated and held no personal grudge against Scotland Yard. 'If my men don't take guns,' he told his superior officer, 'the Irish will fight it out with fists.' In any event, there turned out to be no fight of any kind. The Irish had vacated the two buildings prior to the arrival of Fabian's raiding parties. As Fabian searched one of the dingy flats, he glimpsed something in the fireplace. A closer look revealed a scrap of paper – charred and curled – amongst the ashes. Fabian picked it up between thumb and forefinger, frightened it might crumble in his hands. It was a piece of a letter. By sheer dumb luck, the fire had consumed most of the document, leaving this one small scrap that identified a place where the conspirators were scheduled to meet the following evening.

Fabian recognised the address. It was in a district of London policed by fellow Yard inspector Leonard Crawford.[*] Fabian showed

---

[*] As a superintendent in 1955, Crawford took part in the questioning of Ruth Ellis.

the burned scrap to Crawford, who said the place referenced was a 'grubby little café'. The police hatched a simple plan. An undercover officer would wait in the café and keep an eye out for any gathering of young Irishmen. Fabian and Crawford knew they would easily be identified as police officers, which ruled them out of the operation. A young policewoman – 'pretty and intelligent-eyed' – volunteered for the role. 'It was,' noted Fabian, 'a dangerous job, but she was disguised by an expert and sent off.'

Throughout the late afternoon and early evening, Fabian and Crawford sat by the phone, waiting for the call that would spring them into action. The phone, when it rang on Crawford's desk that night, was a jarring sound that only seemed to heighten the tension. When Crawford answered, the policewoman on the end of the line said she had made contact with the gang. One of the men had bought her a cup of coffee and engaged her in conversation. He told her they had just moved into a new building late the night before in Leinster Gardens. Crawford moved quickly to complete the search warrant and muster a team of officers to raid the lodging house the suspects now called home. They parked the cars a short distance from the building and approached on foot, taking full advantage of the cover of night. Crawford and two of his men made their way, via the building next door, to the rooftop of the gang's hideout. In the street below, an officer banged on the building's front door and ordered those inside to open up. Suddenly, every light in the place went out. The attention of those watching the building from street level was seized by a glimmer of silver up on the roof.

The glass of a skylight slowly being pushed open had caught the light of the moon as three of the building's occupants tried to sneak away. Crawford and two uniformed constables immediately confronted the would-be escapees. The Irishmen had no intention of surrendering quietly. They charged the officers on the rooftop's 'slanting, creaking tiles'. It was a short but desperate struggle as the policemen fought their way back from the roof's edge. There was little the officers on the street could do as they watched the silhouetted figures struggle above. Crawford and his men soon got the better of their assailants, wrestling them to the tiles and slapping them in handcuffs. As Crawford got to his feet, the three Irishmen pleaded to be taken to the police station – a request Crawford had never heard any suspect make in his many years on the force. Indeed, the men seemed desperate to be as far away from the building as they possibly could. Crawford lowered himself through the skylight, suspecting a ticking bomb had been planted on the premises.

He began making his way from one room to another, mindful of the fact that if indeed there was a bomb, he might only have a few minutes remaining before the device detonated. In one room he found a suitcase from which he could just make out the distinct ticking of an alarm clock. Slowly, he opened the case and saw four boxes – each 'packed with sickly-smelling gelignite and clock-detonators'. With steady hands, Crawford went to work dismantling each bomb, slowly removing the wire connecting the clock and the sticky explosive.

The bombings would continue. Banks, bridges, and, in one instance, a newspaper, the *News Chronicle* on Fleet Street, came under fire. The explosives, noted Fabian, 'were home-made affairs … Innocent people were killed, pillar-boxes and mail vans were wrecked, shops and banks shattered. Wild-eyed young Irishmen were arrested and sentenced to long terms of penal servitude, and some were hanged. It was a miserable squabble.' For his bravery in Piccadilly Circus on the night of 24 June 1939, Fabian received two awards. One came from appreciative members of the London underworld, who, upon summoning Fabian to a West End pub several weeks later, gave him 'a beautiful little bronze medal on a blue silk ribbon'. The other award – being of a more prestigious pedigree – was the King's Medal for Gallantry, presented to Fabian in February 1940 during a ceremony at Buckingham Palace. Fabian's place in the history of British law enforcement was now well secured. Heading into the war years, notes one crime historian, 'no Scotland Yard officer was better known than Superintendent Robert Fabian, "Fabian of the Yard"'.

5

THE SUSPECT

Like any good police officer, Constable Michael Lomasney knew the people on his beat. To that end, he was well acquainted with the Potters, seeing them as he did on his routine patrols throughout the area. Albert Potter's behaviour in the field on the night of the killing had certainly puzzled Lomasney, who couldn't understand why a hardened farmer would suddenly be so susceptible to cold weather and the sight of blood.

On the morning of Sunday, 18 February, Lomasney decided to stop by the Potter farm unannounced. He drove from the Warwickshire Constabulary office in Long Marston and arrived at 9.30 a.m. He parked his car in the farmyard and was met at the front door by Lilian Potter, her eyes red and swollen. In a quiet voice, she invited Lomasney in and led him into the kitchen where she began preparing two cups of tea. As she fumbled about, Lomasney asked how she was holding up. The question seemed to grant the permission she needed to yield to her emotions. Turning to face Lomasney, she broke down, her body convulsed by great sobs. She tried to speak but couldn't muster any words. Lomasney, surprised by the outburst, helped Lilian into a chair and did his utmost to calm her down. It took several minutes before she gained control of her breathing and was able to say anything.

Between sobs, she said:

You know we have never had anything to do with the villagers much, and what will they think? They will put it down to Alf. We are worried almost to death. Last night, he woke up – and I knew it was on his mind. You see, he worked for us and it happened on our land, but we cannot account for where Alf was every bit of the day.

Lomasney did his best to comfort Lilian. In a small village, one must expect people to talk – the trick was not to let the wagging tongues get to you. If the Potters simply told investigators all they knew and stuck with the truth, they had nothing to worry about. The words did little to soothe Lilian's emotional state. Deciding it was best to give her time alone, Lomasney left. In the farmyard, he saw Potter emerging from a barn.

'I think you've been talking to the wife too much about this business,' the constable said. 'She is worrying about it.'

Potter simply stared at Lomasney and said nothing. He seemed uncomfortable, glancing nervously about. At last, he mumbled something under his breath – something the constable couldn't make out. 'I believe,' Lomasney would later write in his report, 'he was on the verge of weeping.' Seeing as Potter was not in a talkative mood, Lomasney made his exit. As he walked back to his police car, he couldn't help but brood on how Potter had refused to make eye contact.

※

Two days later, on 20 February, the coroner of Warwickshire County, George Frederick Lodder, held an inquest into Walton's death at the town hall in Stratford-upon-Avon. Pathologist James M. Webster testified the old man had died from shock and severe loss of blood. The scratches on the back of Walton's hands were indicative of someone who had tried to defend themselves. From the positioning of the body in the field, Webster theorised the killer had knocked Walton down, plunged the hayfork through the old man's face and then attacked him with the billhook. The jury reached the expected verdict of 'murder by some person or persons unknown'. Little else was revealed at the hearing, which was adjourned for a month.

That same day, Lomasney returned to The Firs to check up once more on the Potters. He arrived at their place shortly before 6 p.m. that evening and found Alfred Potter in an agitated mood. Why, the farmer wanted to know, had he not been called to give evidence at the coroner's inquest that morning? Lomasney shrugged. Perhaps, he said, investigators had from Potter all they needed. The answer did little to ease Potter's concern. He paced nervously about the room, expressing his ongoing fears about what the villagers must think. This sort of thing could put a man out of business.

'This,' Potter declared with considerable force, 'was the work of a fascist from the camp!'

Lomasney assured Potter the police were going to look at the POW camp in Long Marston and interview the inmates. The investigation was still ongoing, and all relevant avenues would be explored. Perhaps the killer had been careless and left fingerprints on the 'tools used against Walton'. Such a possibility, Lomasney noted, 'had a terrible effect on Mrs Potter. Mr Potter was also greatly affected by the remark.' Indeed, the very thought of it seemed to shock Potter, who appeared on the brink of losing his composure but 'quickly recovered'. As she had done on Lomasney's previous visit, Lilian began to cry. Potter told the constable he had touched the handle of the billhook when he first stumbled upon Walton's body. His intent, he said, had only been to get a clearer look at what had happened.

'I have told the police that,' Potter said. 'I have told them more than once. They knew that.'

Lilian's voice bristled with anger.

'They will have your fingerprints now to blame you for it,' she yelled. 'You fool!'

Potter tried to reassure her and gently chided her for being silly. This was the first Lomasney had heard of Potter touching anything at the crime scene. Being the first officer summoned to the field that night, he wondered why Potter hadn't said anything then. It seemed odd this should come up now. In his statement to Detective Inspector Toombs, shortly after the body's discovery, Potter omitted any mention of touching the billhook – he certainly didn't say anything about it to Fabian and Webb. Was Potter, perhaps guilty in Walton's death, backtracking and building a story to explain why his prints were on a murder weapon? If he was innocent, why make the point of now stressing the fact his prints were on one of the implements? Whatever his reasoning, Potter was doing little to help his cause. His claim to Lomasney and his wife that he had now told police 'more than once' was a lie. The only person he had told prior to this moment was Police Constable West, who had been guarding the crime scene the morning after the murder. When he later sat down with the detectives from Scotland Yard, he never bothered telling them he had returned to the field in the early hours of 15 February.

Increasingly suspicious of Potter's behaviour, Lomasney paid Potter and Lilian a third visit on the evening of Thursday, 22 February. The three of them drove to the Lygon Arms in nearby Chipping Campden for drinks. Originally a sixteenth-century coaching inn, the place was now a pub and inn owned by Potter's father. On the drive home, conversation turned once more to the ongoing investigation. Potter couldn't understand why the men from Scotland Yard were talking to other farm labourers. Lomasney noted that Potter appeared to be very worried. Once back at The Firs, Lilian began discussing the murder and again stressing about its impact on their reputation. Inside the house, her worry once more turned to anger, as she again scolded her husband for touching the handle of the billhook.

'It's all right,' Potter said. 'I have nothing to fear. Anyone might have done the same – and, anyhow, I have told the detectives about it.'

'Are you sure?' Lilian asked. 'Are you sure you told them?'

Potter thought for a moment.

'I don't think they read that bit out to me afterwards,' he finally said, referring to Webb reading back the statement Potter gave on 17 February before asking Potter to sign it. 'I don't remember it if they did. There was such a lot said, but I'm sure I told them.'

He turned to Lomasney.

'Oh, I expect they will see me again,' he said, 'but I'm not worried. I've nothing to fear. I can only tell them the truth.'

Lomasney, for his part, had no doubt Fabian and Webb would be talking with Potter again, for he planned to tell them all he had heard on these recent visits to the farm.

❋

All the while, Fabian and Webb continued pushing forward with their investigation. On the same day as the coroner's inquest, the West Midland Forensic Science Laboratory in Birmingham sent back the results of the forensic analysis of Walton's walking stick, fingernails, and clothing. At his desk, Fabian opened the report and read the following:

<u>Walking stick and hairs removed from it</u>: (Exhibits 1 and 2). The hairs embedded in the bloodstains on this exhibit were microscopically indistinguishable from those of the deceased.

<u>Fingernails of deceased</u>: There was a considerable quantity of soil below each finger nail, and in the soil a large number of fibres were found. The majority of these were identical with similar fibres from the deceased's own clothing, but there were also a number of others, via:

Fibres of reddish-brown wool.
Fibres of blue wool of a varying light shade.
Violet-brown wool and cotton strands.
One fragment of crimson wool.
One piece of green wool.
Some pieces of light yellow to yellow-green wool.

The most prevalent of the above were fibres of blue wool, but it must be borne in mind:

That some of these fibres may have been present in the soil; and
That they may be from other clothing belonging to deceased.

<u>Clothing of the deceased</u>. There were many hairs on this clothing all belonging to the deceased and many cases of inter-change of fibres between his own clothing, but once again some extraneous matter was found:

<u>Jacket</u> (Exhibit 8) On this article were two fairly long yellow woolen fibres, a dark brown piece of wool, and a strand of light blue wool.
<u>Overall trousers</u> (Exhibit 12) Adhering to these was a light blue wool fibre.

The rest of the clothing showed nothing which could definitely be said to have come from a source other than the deceased himself.

Fabian sighed and leaned back in his chair. Nothing in the report seemed to place the investigation on firmer footing. The case posed its own unique challenges. Most victims of homicide are killed by someone they know. In the early stages of an investigation, this often helps centre the focus of an inquiry. People in the city tended to move within limited circles. They had their friends and acquaintances and rarely strayed beyond those social confines. If one dug deep enough, you'd always find some animosity or source of conflict between certain individuals. Village life, Fabian realised, was slightly different. Everyone seemed to know Charles Walton – if not on a deep personal level, then at least by sight. No one Fabian and Webb had spoken to thus far seemed to have any problems with the victim. Fabian noticed that when questioning the villagers, nothing was volunteered freely. They would respond to his questions but never offer anything more beyond what he was asking. He was merely an outsider, prying and asking questions. Never mind the purpose of his business. It was also odd the villagers expressed no concern for their own safety. An old man had been slaughtered in the most gruesome fashion in a local field, and there seemed to be no fear a madman might be on the loose. And so while the residents of Lower Quinton were cooperating with investigators, Fabian didn't believe they were being entirely open.

Since arriving in Lower Quinton, he had struggled to formulate any sort of motive behind the killing. Indeed, it seemed a purely senseless act. Robbery seemed the most plausible explanation, for what other reason could there be for butchering a harmless old man who kept to himself? The fact Walton's clothes appeared to have been rifled through gave credence to such reasoning. In her statement to Fabian and Webb several days prior, Edith said her uncle was a frugal man. Although he had an account with Midland Bank in Stratford, she didn't know how much he had saved. Walton had a will, and Edith assumed the majority of his estate would be left to her. A search of Walton's cottage had revealed no hidden stash of money and nothing of any great value. Inquiries made around the village seemed to indicate that some residents thought Walton was a man of substantial means. From 1937 to the autumn of 1944, Walton had worked for Frederick Frost, the owner of Magdalen Farm in Lower Quinton. Frost told Fabian he paid Walton no less than £3 a week over the course of those seven years. He eventually laid Walton off due to the old man's deteriorating health. As Fabian put down in his case notes, Walton 'was a man of frugal habits. His rent was but three shillings a week and his total outgoings at the most cannot be estimated at more than £2 per week. Walton did not smoke and seldom visited a public house.' His spendthrift

not the usual meaning of this word

ways, coupled with a £3-per-week salary over seven years, must have surely meant Walton was relatively well off.

Magdalen Farm worker Horace Yates related an interesting story to Fabian.

'Some two years ago,' he said when questioned:

> I was working with Charles Walton when I lost a pound note. I mentioned this, and Walton said, 'You shouldn't carry money about with you. I don't; only a few shillings.' He did go on to say something about not being short of £200 or £300. He didn't say where it was.

Another farm worker who witnessed the exchange corroborated the story. Other locals the detectives questioned were of the same opinion that Walton had a considerable amount of money stashed away somewhere. If such a belief was common throughout the village, then perhaps someone had killed Walton in a failed attempt to get at his money. Fabian and Webb paid a visit one afternoon to Midland Bank on Chapel Street in Stratford. The manager showed Fabian Walton's financial records. Through Edith, Fabian knew that Walton had received £297 upon the death of his wife in 1927. Early the following year, he took £200 of that money and deposited it into his Midland Bank account. According to the records produced by the bank manager, it appeared Walton received £44 in 1936 from a benevolent club he had joined several years prior. And while he was gainfully employed as a farm labourer throughout this period, and the years immediately preceding his murder, his account balance was only £2 15s 6d. When taking into account 30s Fabian had found in Walton's dresser and another thirty shillings found in a purse in his bedroom, Walton's total cash assets at the time of his death were no more than £5. It didn't make sense. Fabian ran a finger down Walton's account registry and saw the old man's savings had dwindled from £227 in 1929 to the present amount of just over £2. So where was all of Walton's money? The records revealed no large withdrawals, but they also showed few deposits. With the wages he made during this period, he could have easily covered his living expenses and had money left over for savings. Fabian could only theorise that Walton 'had secreted the money somewhere'.

In pursuing financial gain as a possible motive, Fabian had merely uncovered more questions. Edith was certainly at a loss to explain the missing funds. Looking for an alternative avenue of exploration, Fabian considered the ferocity of the attack. Cuts and bruises on Walton's hands suggested he put up some kind of a struggle. Although there was no blood or skin tissue beneath Walton's nails, wasn't it possible he inflicted some sort of injury on his assailant? Fabian dispatched officers to check area hospitals, doctors' surgeries, and casualty wards for anyone who may have been treated the day of the murder 'for cuts or injuries to the hands or head'. The inquiries would turn up nothing.

Meanwhile, the canvassing of Lower Quinton and the surrounding area continued. Fabian wanted to know if anyone was near the scene of the crime when it took place. He began visiting local farms to see if there were any other workers in the fields that morning. His inquiries brought him into contact with a labourer at Meon Hill Farm and another at a farm in Upper Quinton, both of whom claimed to have seen British soldiers on Meon Hill the morning of the murder. One soldier appeared to be collecting booby traps left for rabbits; the other was seen walking away from the hill in the direction of Lower Quinton. The information presented the first solid lead to come Fabian's way. Taking the investigation to the army barracks in Warwick, he learned the soldiers on the hill that day were Lieutenant Alan Edwards of the 23rd ITC, Sergeant George Mills and Lance Corporal George Hobbis of the Royal Warwickshire Regiment. Edwards was in charge of manoeuvres on Meon Hill the day Walton died, while Hobbis and Mills were on the slopes removing booby traps set the day before. The soldiers left the hill at about 11 a.m. and returned to their barracks. They saw nothing out of the ordinary that morning, and all their alibis checked out.

Impatient for a lead, Fabian returned to the police station in Stratford and reread the forensics report. Something, this time, didn't seem quite right. He read the report again. Included with the document was an inventoried list of the clothing items examined. Among them was a grey jacket, grey waistcoat, a shirt, and a blue cardigan. Walton, a frail old man, was susceptible to the cold as it caused his rheumatism to flare up. Fabian opened his desk drawer and withdrew two folders: one containing the statement given by Edith Walton on 16 February; the other Potter's statement from 17 February. He flipped through the typed pages of Edith's statement and found what he was looking for:

> On Wednesday the 14th February 1945, my uncle went off to work as usual at about half-past-eight ... He was dressed as he usually was when he went hedging. He had a tweed jacket and a pair of grey flannel trousers on. He was wearing a pair of blue overall trousers over his flannels. He also had a waistcoat on which matched the jacket and a heather mixture cardigan. He wore a flannel body belt, a flannel shirt, and a cotton shirt which was almost white ... He had a cap, a pair of black boots and knitted socks.

Indeed, this was a man who preferred to keep warm. If the weather was cold, he didn't venture out. He now scanned Potter's statement and stopped at the relevant passage:

> On the morning of Wednesday the 14th February 1945, at about ten past twelve, I went across to 'Cacks Leys' a field on my farm, to see to some sheep and feed some calves. When I got there it was twenty past twelve, and I saw Walton working at the hedge in the next field. He was about 500 yards away and was in his shirtsleeves. I am quite sure of this. This was the first occasion I had seen him in his shirtsleeves since he had been hedge cutting, and I thought to myself, 'He's getting on with it today.'

If Potter really did see someone working in their shirtsleeves, it could not have been Walton. Was Potter simply mistaken by what he saw, or did he see someone else entirely, perhaps the murderer in the act of killing the old man? On the morning of 23 February, Lomasney reported to Fabian at the Stratford-upon-Avon Police Station to discuss the night the body was found and what the constable believed to be Potter's strange behaviour in the field. Lomasney said Potter seemed repulsed by the sight of blood on Walton's walking stick. This might seem a natural reaction for one not used to gore, but Potter made his living slaughtering animals and, in Lomasney's words, 'is accustomed to the sight of blood'. The weather that evening was cold and promised an early morning frost. Not until he saw the blood-spattered walking stick, did the temperature suddenly become an issue for Potter. He began complaining about the weather – a strange subject for one to take issue with considering the circumstances.

'His complaint of feeling cold,' said Lomasney, 'I considered a strange excuse from one who was used to attending to animals at all hours and in all kinds of weather, especially as the murdered man was his own employee and had been murdered on his land.'

The constable also thought it odd that Potter – saying he was 'famished' – left the crime scene prior to the arrival of detectives from the Stratford Police. While Fabian also thought Potter's timing was certainly questionable, so too was the man's reason for leaving. What sort of person, having only just discovered the brutalised body of a co-worker, would have food on their mind? Fabian continued listening as Lomasney went on to detail the past three evenings spent in the company of the Potters and all Potter had said, including how he had touched one of the murder weapons. Startled to hear of Potter's admission, Fabian called the farmer at The Firs and asked him to come to the police station that afternoon to clear a few things up.

Potter, although certainly a person of interest, had not been considered a suspect – until now. The farm implements were his, so his fingerprints would naturally be on them. Why make a point of saying he had touched one of the handles at the murder scene? Fabian did not want Potter in the comfortable surroundings of his own home. Conducting the interview at the station would lend extra weight to the proceedings. Potter, in unfamiliar territory, might slip up and reveal something. The farmer, as one might expect, did not seem overly pleased by his summons when he arrived later that afternoon. 'Morose' would be the word used by Fabian in his official report.

'We'd like to ask you some more questions, Mr Potter,' Fabian said, leading his new suspect into an interrogation room. Webb was sitting at a table with Potter's previous statement typed and arranged neatly in front of him. A woman sat in the corner, her hands poised over a typewriter, ready to transcribe the conversation. 'We're hoping you can clarify a few things.'

Potter took a seat. Fabian sat alongside Webb, who read the farmer's statement taken six days earlier. When Webb finished reading, Fabian asked if there was anything Potter might like to change or add.

'I find that there are one or two mistakes,' Potter said, nodding. 'I want to put these right.'

'Start from the beginning,' said Fabian, 'and walk us through your day again.'

Potter, speaking slowly, said he spent the morning of 14 February in a field checking on his livestock, after which he returned to the farmhouse for a short break and read the newspaper.* Although unsure of the time, he told Fabian and Webb he then went out to the barn to help Charles Batchelor, the cowman, pulp some mangolds. The two men worked together for no more than ten minutes before stepping outside to check the time on the church clock, which looked down into the farmyard. It was just coming up on 1p.m., at which point both men went off to their respective homes for lunch.

'And how long were you in the house?' asked Fabian.

'About an hour and ten minutes,' Potter replied.

Fabian couldn't help but notice how precise Potter was with the time. Continuing his statement, Potter said he paid Batchelor another visit after lunch and made arrangements to remove a dead heifer from a local creek known as Doomsday Brook. Once the animal's corpse had been dealt with, Potter spent the remainder of the day – from three onwards – milking cows. At 5.50 p.m., he returned home for his tea. Shortly thereafter, Edith and Harry Beasley knocked on his door, inquiring as to the whereabouts of Charles Walton.

'Do you mind walking us through that again?' asked Fabian.

Potter said:

What I have previously told you about Miss Walton calling on me with Mr Beasley and all going up to the field to find Mr Walton's body is quite true, but I want to add that when Beasley and I arrived at the body we just had a look at it but did not touch anything. As Mr Beasley was about to take Miss Walton away he said to me, 'You had better have a look to make sure he is gone.' I then walked up to the body and caught hold of the trouncing hook by the handle at about the middle. I found it was firmly fixed and then left it alone. I am quite sure I did not touch anything else. Mr Beasley

---

* He makes no mention of seeing Walton working in a neighbouring field.

was walking away with Miss Walton when I touched the trouncing hook handle and I don't suppose he saw what I did.

Fabian placed a cardboard box on the table and pulled out a blood-ied shirt and cardigan.

'In your previous statement,' Fabian said, 'you told us you saw Charles Walton in the field, working in his shirtsleeves. These are the clothes Walton was wearing when he died. Are you sure the man you saw that morning was, in fact, Charles Walton?'

Potter shook his head.

'I realise I could not have seen him working in his shirtsleeves,' he said. 'I am certain, however, that there was somebody in shirtsleeves at about the spot where Mr Walton ought to have been working.'

Fabian, still wondering about Walton's finances, broached the subject with Potter. In his statement on 17 February, Potter said he had paid Walton £2 15s for a fortnight's work four days before the murder. There had been no record at Midland Bank of Walton ever making a deposit in that amount. In and of itself, that was not abnor-mal – but the overall lack of deposits remained a nagging puzzle. When questioned presently about paying Walton his wages, Potter surprised Fabian with a confession. The final amount Potter paid Walton on 10 February was for one week's work, not two.

'Some weeks I have drawn wages for Mr Walton when he has not been at work,' Potter said quietly:

My books will show that he had wages every week whereas, in fact, he did not always have wages as he didn't work in very bad weather. There had been occasions when Mr Walton had asked me for wages due to him and I hadn't had the money to pay him, as I had spent it. I would then pay him later in the week. The last occasion of this sort I remember was just before Christmas 1944.

The admission was relevant, for although Potter's offence was argu-ably a minor one, it revealed a criminal streak in his character. In his previous statement to the Yard men, Potter said he merely ran the farm, while his father owned the business. In short, Potter was stealing from his own family. The overall statement was striking for another reason – though it was one to which Fabian, at this point in the investigation, remained oblivious. Potter had made no mention of his visit to the crime scene the morning after the killing. He had not mentioned it in his first statement to Fabian and Webb, nor had he said anything about it to Lomasney, though he had plenty of opportunity to do so. When coupled with his admission regarding the stealing of Walton's wages, Potter's lack of transparency reveals a true manipulative streak.

Fabian had spent decades interrogating suspects, reading body language, and noting their emotional responses. Potter seemed to loiter only in the dull end of the emotional spectrum, appearing nothing but downbeat through the entire questioning. It was the same front he put forward in his previous statement. As such, Fabian found him hard to read – though he believed the farmer was putting on an act. In his official report, Fabian suggested there was more to Potter than met the eye:

> When interviewed, Potter has always appeared morose and sullen – and even when closely interrogated has never lost his temper or become other than respectful. He is unkempt and would appear, on the surface, to be dull-witted, but I am convinced he is far from that. He is a man of considerable strength and, in my opinion, is an extremely cunning individual.

Potter, a man of considerable girth, would certainly have been able to overpower Walton. Fabian finished the proceedings by taking from Potter his workman's clothes, which included a pair of Bedford cord breeches. Fabian examined the clothes, running his hands over the fabric and holding them up under the light for better inspection. Even as he did this, Potter showed no signs of concern.

'You may find some blood on the knees,' Potter said. 'I got it there when I took a calf from a cow last Monday.'

Fabian counted backwards in his head. The Monday would have been 19 February, five days after Walton's death. With nothing more to ask, Fabian let the farmer go.

❋

Potter's description of what he was doing between noon and 1 p.m. on 14 February had changed since his first statement to Inspector Toombs on the night of the murder. On that occasion, he said he left the College Arms at noon and went to check on livestock in a field adjoining the one in which Walton was working. There, he supposedly saw the old man busy with his hedging duties. Fabian found it curious that Potter, again, had been very specific about the time he left the pub. Most often, people recalling the details of their day spoke in generalities when it came to time. Potter seemed to have made note of the hour. If this first statement was true, then it means Potter saw Walton – or someone he thought to be Walton – no earlier than 12.10 p.m., for it took about ten minutes to walk from the pub to the field. In his statement to Fabian and Webb on 17 February, Potter said it was 12.10 p.m. when he left the pub – and 12.20 p.m. when he arrived in the field and saw the man he believed to be Walton standing still in the next field over. Now, there were two discrepancies. As Fabian wrote in his case report, 'Potter's story gradually change[d] from seeing Charles working at hedge cutting at 12.10 p.m. to seeing a man standing stationary at 12.30 p.m.'

So did Potter see Walton busy at work or the killer standing over the body? That latter option seems unlikely as Potter, in his first statement to Fabian and Webb, said the distance between the spot where he supposedly saw Walton working and the spot where the body was eventually found constituted about half-an-hour's cutting work. As Fabian would note in the case file, 'If the man who Potter saw was not Walton it would be interesting to know who did the half-an-hour's work on the hedge.'

Potter, in his first statement to Fabian and Webb, said he would have gone over and chatted with Walton but had to remove a dead heifer from a ditch. He told the detectives he left the field and went straight home, getting there at 12.40 p.m., then went to examine the cow. Now, in the version of events he had detailed just minutes ago, his story had changed. Fabian read through the transcribed statement and found the relevant part: 'I went home and looked at the paper for about five minutes ... I then ... helped Batchelor ... for about five minutes ... I looked at the church clock. It was just one o'clock.' Fabian, in his official report, described the importance of the various misalignments in Potter's statements:

The aforementioned discrepancies are most significant for they affect the very time when Charles Walton was probably being murdered. Potter inferred in his statement of the 17th February, 1945, that it was only pressure of work that prevented him going over to Walton at 12.20 p.m. on the 14th February whilst in his statement of the 23rd February, he admits he went straight home and read the paper. The business of attending to the heifer in the ditch was not carried out until about 3 p.m. that day. Potter is undoubtedly lying about his actions at this critical time but the reason for these lies can, for the present, only be a matter of conjecture.

Fabian wanted to know more about what Potter did in the field the night the body was found. It was odd the man seemed to be going out of his way to let police know he touched the trouncing hook. Lomasney, in previous conversation with Fabian, had said Potter never once mentioned it the night of the murder and only brought it up when he, Lomasney, broached the subject of fingerprints on one of his recent visits to The Firs. Two days after arriving in the Cotswolds to launch their investigation, Fabian and Webb had questioned Harry Beasley, who, with Edith, was in the field with Potter when the gruesome discovery was made. Potter had said he only touched the trouncing hook after Beasley told him to make sure Walton was dead. In his statement, however, Beasley never mentioned any such exchange taking place. It was time to question Beasley again.

6

AN UNYIELDING PUZZLE

On 24 February, Fabian and Webb made the drive from Stratford to Lower Quinton. Not for the first time, Fabian pondered how they seemed a world away from the bomb-ravaged streets of London, with their sandbags and surface air-raid shelters. Here, everything seemed, in contrast, so pristine: the fields bright green and the thatched-roof cottages free of black soot. There were no pillboxes, no piles of rubble, or structures surrounded by barbed wire. That's not to say the war hadn't intruded on local life. Thousands of children from the cities had been evacuated to the country and placed in area homes, far from friends and family. Although the Cotswolds were spared the horror of large-scale air attacks, searchlights and anti-aircraft guns were placed on high ground throughout the region. Prior to the Allied invasion of Europe, a lot of rural land throughout the district had given way to 'training and transit camps used by thousands of troops'. British servicemen were the predominant military presence in the early days of the war, but now American troops in the thousands populated the area. The grounds of local country manors were turned over to the war effort and used to house soldiers. Many fields were bulldozed and flattened for the construction of airfields. At night, the sound of bombers thrummed high in the darkness, as young men, passing over sleeping villages, winged their way to some unknown fate. War had touched every corner of Britain. That an old, defenceless man should die such a heinous death against a national backdrop of so much killing and destruction made Walton's murder seem all the more pointless.

Fabian watched the countryside roll pass the car. He was operating in unfriendly territory. The West End was his 'office table and work-bench'. He would later write:

> The art of being a good policeman in a metropolis like London, consists of knowing everybody and winning their friendship; so that when ... situations arise ... it needs no painstaking Sherlock Holmes work with magnifying glass on the carpet: one simply knows that every skein and thread of the sensitive web that makes up the secret life of London will all lead back to you.

Here, amidst the rural folk and the customs of the country, Fabian knew no one. He had no leverage to exercise. Nearly a week in the area and he had no solid lead upon which to build his investigation. He needed that one loose thread; something he could pull to unravel the whole sordid mystery. All he had were the discrepancies in Potter's statements. That didn't amount to evidence of committing murder, but it did nothing to establish the man's innocence.

Webb turned the car into the yard at Henney's Farm. In his initial statement to the detectives, Beasley had said he saw no one touch the body that night in the field. Potter, of course, had just told Fabian he touched the trouncing hook after Beasley left to walk Edith home. It was, for Potter, convenient timing. Beasley emerged from a barn and greeted Fabian and Webb as they got out of the car. Fabian said he wanted Beasley to walk them through the discovery of the body one more time.

'When Mr Potter and I first saw the body of Charles Walton, I said, "He's gone," or something to that effect,' Beasley said. 'It was after that that Mr Potter called to Peachey and I waited until Mr Potter had sent Peachey away for assistance before I turned to take Miss Walton home.'

'And did you ask Potter to make sure Walton was dead, or see him touch anything?' Fabian asked.

Beasley said:

> It was clear to me Charles Walton was dead. It was then that I said, 'I had better get Edith back home.' This was the last thing I said to Mr Potter except, perhaps, 'Do you want me to bring

anything back?' Some mention was also made of a stretcher and help to get the body down. I then took Edith away. I did not say to Mr Potter, 'You better make sure to have a look to make sure he is gone.' I am sure that whilst I was there he did not touch either the body, the trouncing hook, or the hay fork. I had no doubt from the first glance at the body that Charles Walton was dead. When I first said, 'He's gone,' Mr Potter either replied, 'Yes,' or nodded his head. I am confident that Mr Potter realised that Charles Walton was dead from the very first.

Fabian and Webb exchanged a glance. Beasley had no reason to lie. Why would Potter make a claim one could so easily disprove? What did it say about the man? As Fabian did not believe Potter to be stupid, perhaps the farmer took a dim view of the police. But surely he would know follow-up questions would be asked and statements would be checked – then checked again. Although there was no evidence to suggest Potter had killed Walton, his actions since the killing made him the most obvious suspect. As Fabian would write in his official report:

> Potter's story of handling the trouncing hook is most unsatisfactory. Although he has endeavoured to lead people into believing that he mentioned it to police soon after the murder, there can be no doubt that he, in fact, did not do so until the question of fingerprints was raised by PC Lomasney. Potter has also endeavoured to explain in a convincing way how he came to touch the trouncing hook, but Mr Beasley is quite sure that it did not occur in the manner suggested by Potter. Whatever the reason, Potter has gone to great pains to explain away any of his fingerprints, which might be found upon the weapons with which Charles Walton was murdered.

What Potter had no way of knowing, however, and what Fabian had no intention of telling him, was that no fingerprints were found on either the trouncing hook or the pitchfork.

✳

Charles Henry Batchelor, a 37-year-old farm labourer, lived in a small house on Friday Street. He had worked for L.L. Potter and Sons for the past three years – ever since moving to Lower Quinton – and for

Alfred Potter, specifically, for three months. He invited Fabian and Webb in when they knocked at his door and led them into a small sitting room. Potter had prominently referred to Batchelor in his most recent statement. Batchelor, in turn, seemed to corroborate everything Potter had said. He told Fabian and Webb he first saw Potter on the day in question at 10 a.m. that morning, just prior to lunch. The next time he crossed paths with his employer was at 12.40 p.m. when Potter entered the mixing house, where Batchelor was busy pulping mangolds.

'You're very specific about the time,' Fabian said.

Batchelor said:

I remember it exactly, because I asked Mr Potter the time, and he replied, 'I'm not sure, but it must be getting on.' He helped me with the mangolds, and we then both walked into the yard and looked at the church clock. It was 1 p.m. Mr Potter then went towards his house, as far as I know to have his dinner.

The two men spoke again at 2.15 p.m. that afternoon and discussed how they were going to remove the dead heifer from the ditch on Potter's property, Batchelor said. Potter went to a neighbouring farm to inquire about borrowing a tractor and returned roughly ten minutes later. Shortly after that, he left to deal with the heifer and returned to The Firs at 4 p.m. The two men then worked in the milking sheds until 6 p.m., when Batchelor went home for the evening. The times seemed to align with those stated by Potter in his statement, although Potter said he had been back at the farm by 3 p.m. after removing the heifer from the brook.

'Did you know Charles Walton?' asked Fabian.

'I have known Mr Walton for about twelve months and always found him to be a happy and jovial type of man,' Batchelor said. 'He seemed quite contented and always minded his own business.'

Batchelor, guided by Fabian's questions, said he never heard Walton discuss personal finances and didn't, as far as he knew, walk about carrying large sums of money. The only item of any possible value the old man seemed to keep on him was the pocket watch. Asked if he ever saw Walton working in shirtsleeves, Batchelor said he hadn't. In regards to Potter, the farmer had always paid Batchelor his wages on time and never owed him money. And what of Potter in general, Fabian inquired, did Batchelor know the man to have any mental issues? Had his demeanour changed since the killing?

Batchelor replied:

Mr Potter has seemed very upset and worried since this affair happened. When talking to me about it, he appeared to be in a quandary as to who could have done it. Since I've known Mr Potter, I've never known him to be seriously ill, and he has always been kind and generous towards me. He has a bit of a temper, but no more than the rest of us. I have never known or heard of him suffering from loss of memory or brainstorms. His attitude is the same towards us all. As far as I know, Mr Potter and Mr Walton had always been quite friendly.

Recalling Potter's earlier statements in which he said he was in the College Arms before noon, Fabian asked Batchelor if his employer had problems with alcohol.

'Mr Potter likes his glass of beer like the rest of us,' Batchelor said. 'I have been in his company in public houses on many occasions but have never known him really drunk.'

Outside, the afternoon sky was beginning to threaten rain.

'What do you think?' asked Webb.

'Batchelor corroborates in detail Potter's statement as to his movements after he saw Walton that morning,' said Fabian, 'but it's curious that Potter, having such a witness, didn't mention the mangold pulping in his earlier statements. It may be possible that Potter bided his time to make sure that Batchelor was prepared to vouch for his movements at that critical time.'

Over the following days, Fabian and Webb sought to corroborate Potter's movements on the morning of the murder. Joseph Stanley, owner of White Cross Farm in Lower Quinton, told the detectives Potter came over that morning to castrate two of Stanley's calves shortly after 11 a.m. The two men walked to the College Arms when the work was done for some liquid refreshment. Stanley drank one pint of Guinness, while Potter downed two. They were in the pub for no more than a quarter of an hour, from 11.45 a.m. to noon, after which they returned to Stanley's farm to inspect his tractor and discuss the removal of the dead heifer from the ditch. They parted company a few minutes later. A farm labourer named John Field, busy that morning carting straw from the village to a farm on Meon Hill, told Fabian he saw Potter and Stanley inspecting the tractor in Stanley's garage shortly after the noon hour. Field said he worked until 2 p.m. that afternoon.

Field told the detectives:

> During the whole of this time, I did not see a stranger about. The field in which Charlie Walton was killed was in the half-circle surrounding the route I took. I did not see anything out of the ordinary. I did not see anyone go across the fields of Potter's farm that morning. I would have had a full view of the field where the body was found.

✳

The College Arms is a country pub in the traditional style, with thick stone walls, burning fire place, and knotted beamed ceilings. The building, situated near the small village green, dates back to the sixteenth century. The pub's name reportedly originates from Oxford University's Magdalen College, which once owned land in the area. Supposedly, it's the only pub in England allowed to use the college's coat of arms. Fabian enjoyed pubs. In London, he revelled in the social environs of a few select drinking establishments. Among his favourites he counted The Prospect of Whitby at Wapping Wall and the Fitzroy Tavern in Charlotte Street, both bustling with the noise and energy of city life, the latter boasting a wartime notice on the wall that read, 'Business as usual during alterations to Germany.' The College Arms, by contrast, was quiet when he and Webb entered the premises. The few locals hunched at the bar nodded in polite greeting then returned to their drinks. Over a couple of pints, Fabian and Webb weighed the merits of Potter as suspect.

Potter had an alibi for most of the day, with one exception: What was he doing between the time he left Stanley's farm shortly after noon and when Charles Batchelor saw him at The Firs forty-plus minutes later? Batchelor had put the time at 12.40 p.m., telling the detectives it was 1 p.m. when he and Potter checked the church clock after pulping some mangolds. Potter, however, said he only helped Batchelor for five minutes before they checked the clock, meaning it was most likely later than 12.40 p.m. when Batchelor saw him. It would have been ample time to walk from The Firs to the field where Walton was hedging, commit the crime, then return to the farm and clean up before carrying on with the day's business. By his own admission, Potter said he was in the field adjoining the one in which Walton was working at 12.20 p.m. He then returned to the farmhouse and read the newspaper for five minutes. It struck Fabian as odd one would sit for a mere five minutes to read the paper. Was the farmer padding his account, attempting to account for lost time?

Fabian had neither seen nor heard anything to suggest Potter was a man of violent disposition. Certainly, Fabian had worked homicides where the killer lashed out in a sudden fit of rage or passion, but the Walton murder went beyond that, so extreme was the level of violence. And there was still the nagging question of motive. Fabian's mind kept circling back to money. Potter had admitted to stealing Walton's pay on past occasions and being unable to pay him on time. Maybe it had happened again and the old man called Potter on it. Perhaps Walton threatened to make a fuss about it or go to Potter's father and report him. Another alternative was Potter told Walton he would have his pay at a later date but was unable to come up with the cash. Scared of the consequences, Potter deemed it prudent to rid himself of Walton. Maybe Potter had debts elsewhere and, hearing Walton supposedly carried large sums of money about, killed the old man for financial gain. There was obviously a reason the victim's clothing was disarranged. On the other hand, there was no suggestion from anyone that Potter or Walton ever quarrelled.

Money issues seemed to be a common theme with Potter. In their canvassing of Lower Quinton, Fabian and Webb had discovered Walton wasn't the only one who had trouble with Potter when it came to wages. A former employee named George Purnell, who had worked at Potter's farm for roughly five years, told the detectives that Potter was a man of unpleasant temperament and unscrupulous business practices.

'He was not a good man to work under and frequently threatened to give me the sack and turn me out of my cottage which was on his land,' said Purnell, now a labourer at White Cross Farm. 'He would never lend a hand no matter how busy we were, but would only grumble if not enough was being done.'

'Did you have any issues with being paid on time?' asked Fabian.

'Mr Potter would not pay me the proper overtime rate and would only pay me for four days holiday instead of seven,' he said:

I have asked him about the extra money which he owes me and have written to him about it. I did not get any satisfaction and have placed the matter in the hands of the War Agriculture Committee. He always paid me my money on a Saturday, but not all that I was entitled to. He was a bad-tempered man and a heavy drinker. He would grumble and order me about especially when he was in drink.

Fabian finished the contents of his glass and pulled his pipe and a pouch of tobacco from the pocket of his grey trench coat. Potter might have been a bastard, but that did not necessarily make him a murderer. Fabian tamped the tobacco in the bowl, lit a match, and pondered the brutality of the crime. It had been pure overkill. If Potter was the murderer, why had he gone to such violent extremes? One could have easily killed a man in Walton's deteriorated state with their bare hands or a well-placed blow with one of Walton's walking sticks. Why beat the old man, stab him through the face, and then slash his throat? Perhaps the gruesome nature of the killing was meant to serve as a distraction. Police would think a mad man was on the prowl, for who would believe a local resident to be capable of such an atrocity? Then again, no one in Lower Quinton seemed too concerned by any such prospect. Is that because they knew who did it? It seemed impossible that in a village of no more than 500 people, there wasn't someone who knew something.

No one seemed to have much to say in regards to suspect or victim. In his first statement to Fabian and Webb, Potter mentioned a man named George Higgins, whom he believed to be Walton's 'only friend'. If Higgins was indeed close to Walton, perhaps he was privy to information others were not. Questioning Higgins, Fabian told Webb over their empty glasses, would be their next order of business.

✳

'I have known Charles Walton all my life. We went to school together and have been good friends ever since,' Higgins told Fabian the following day. It was the morning of 24 February. Higgins was 72 and – as had been the case with Walton – still worked odd jobs at local farms. Currently, he was lending a hand at Allan Valender's farm:

I last saw Charles at Christmas. In the summer, I often went for a walk with him on Sunday evenings. For a number of years in the winter, I have been employed with Charles Walton cutting hedges. This is the first winter for a long time that I haven't with him.

They were standing in one of Valender's fields. From their vantage point, they could see the field in which Walton had been killed. The wind was cold and the air was damp. Fabian, his hands thrust deep in the pockets of his coat, spoke around his pipe.

'Did Walton ever work in his shirtsleeves?'

'When hedging, Charles Walton was always a man to get on with his work and not stand about,' Higgins said. 'I cannot think for a moment that he would ever work in his shirtsleeves in the winter.'

'Did he ever carry large sums of money on him?' asked Webb.

'I have never known him to carry any money when he was at work,' Higgins replied. 'He might have had an odd shilling but this I doubt very much because he never spent any and would know he wouldn't want any in the fields. I am fairly certain he wouldn't carry pound notes with him.'

Fabian looked across the fields. The hedgerows rustled in the breeze and the countryside, in the gunmetal light of a winter's day, looked bleak. Not for the first time, Fabian marvelled at the audacity of the killer, striking in open space in broad daylight.

Higgins said:

My eyesight is not so good now, so I cannot see across the fields far – but I must say I haven't seen any strangers across the fields for a long time, not even last summer when I was working in the fields close to where Charles Walton was killed. I can also say that I haven't seen any Italians across the fields. I have seen plenty about the roads in the village.

'And Walton never mentioned having a quarrel with anyone?' Fabian asked. 'Perhaps issues with a past employer?'

'Charles has never told me that he had trouble with anyone,' Higgins said. 'Being his best friend, I think he would have told me if he had done so. He hasn't spoken about any of the farmers he has worked for.'

'Would Walton talk to anyone he encountered in the fields?'

'I don't think he would speak to anyone he saw in the fields unless it was to pass the time of day with them. If they were on the side of the hedge, I don't think he would bother to speak to them unless they spoke to him first.'

Circling back to money, Fabian asked, 'Was anyone in debt to Walton?'

'I think he would have told me if he had lent money to anyone,' Higgins said. 'I should have expected him to have told me if anyone owed him money – but, of course, I haven't seen him since Christmas. If Walton had any money, I think it would be in the bank. He has altered a lot if he carried any amount on him.'

Exploring other avenues, Fabian asked Higgins if he ever saw Italian prisoners or poachers wandering Meon Hill. The old man said he saw neither, adding Walton never mentioned seeing anything.

'I don't think he would be the type to order a poacher off Mr Potter's land,' Higgins said, 'and certainly not the type of man to fall out with anyone.'

'Did he ever carry a means of protection when working?' asked Webb.

Higgins shook his head. 'Years ago, Walton always carried a sporting gun. He was a very good shot, but he hadn't carried his gun for years.'

Fabian almost felt foolish asking the old man to account for his movements on the day of the murder, but over the years he had learned to rule nothing out. Higgins said he started work at Valender's farm at 8.30 a.m. that morning in the barn behind the bakery. He finished his day at 4 p.m.

'The field where Charles Walton was killed is between 200 and 300 yards away from the barn,' Higgins said. 'To the best of my recollection, I did not see anyone while I was at work that day.'

The detectives thanked Higgins for his time and returned to the Stratford Police Station. Indeed, the barn in which Higgins was working on 14 February was a short distance from the crime scene.

Fabian estimated it to be closer to 300 yards. It would have been easy for Higgins to walk unnoticed from the bakery to the field, kill Walton, and return to work without being missed. Fabian, however, quickly dismissed any such notion. Higgins walked with a cane and, like Walton, was small in stature. 'There is no evidence other than that he was always on the friendliest terms with the deceased,' Fabian wrote in his official report. 'It would be difficult to imagine that this old man could have committed a crime of such savagery as the murder of Charles Walton.'

✳

Police considered several other suspects as the investigation wore on, only to quickly rule them out. From a legal standpoint, this would benefit investigators if they made an arrest in the case. Should Potter come to trial for murder, the defence couldn't say Fabian focussed solely on the farmer. One person who came under suspicion was an English army private stationed at the Long Marston Garrison. In addition to the Italian POWs housed there, the garrison was home to 3,093 soldiers of the Royal Engineers and the Pioneer Corps. The private in question was a man named Thomas Davies of the Pioneer Corps, who served as the camp's rat-catcher. Some in the village considered him 'an unscrupulous type of person,' always looking to make easy money. He was frequently spotted wandering the fields around Meon Hill. Farmer Thomas Russell told Fabian that on the day of the murder, he saw Davies hurrying down a lane bordering the fields near the murder site. He seemed to be walking as if in a rush to get somewhere, Russell said. 'You look like you're up to something,' Russell said to Davies, who did not respond and scurried on his way. When questioned by Fabian at the Long Marston barracks, Davies, married and a father of six, said he spent the day at a local farm, laying rat poison and attempting to catch rabbits. With his alibi verified by a half-dozen witnesses, Fabian scratched Davies' name off the suspect list.

Also considered a suspect – if only briefly – was a tramp known locally as 'Ginger', due to his red hair and beard. Identified as 55-year-old Frederick Sandford, 'Ginger' was known to wander the area, sleep in the fields, and do the occasional odd job at one of the local farms. He was seen in the fields the morning of the murder – but, as with Davies, others accounted for his whereabouts at the time of the killing. Undiscouraged, Fabian considered all possible alternatives in his hunt for the killer, noting in his official report, 'A careful check was made on all mental defectives living in the locality and missing from nearby institutions on the day in question, but as far as can be ascertained none of them has any connection with the murder.' More than 400 British servicemen on leave the day Walton died were tracked down and questioned. All were cleared. The more people investigators absolved of any involvement in the crime, the greater Fabian's interest in Potter grew.

Chief Inspector Robert Fabian. In the 1940s, there was perhaps no detective as famous as the redoubtable 'Fabian of the Yard'. The Charles Walton murder proved to be a rare failure for the seasoned investigator.

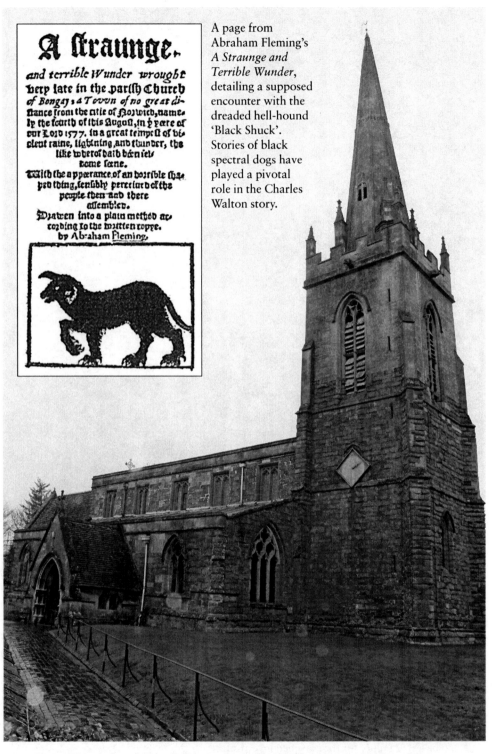

A Straunge,

and terrible Wunder wrought very late in the parish Church of Bongay, a Towne of no great distance from the citie of Norwich, namely the fourth of this August, in ye yeere of our Lord 1577. in a great tempest of violent raine, lightning, and thunder, the like wherof hath been sieldome seene.

With the appearance of an horrible shaped thing, sensibly perceiued of the people then and there assembled.

Drawen into a plaine method according to the written coppye.

by Abraham Fleming.

A page from Abraham Fleming's *A Straunge and Terrible Wunder*, detailing a supposed encounter with the dreaded hell-hound 'Black Shuck'. Stories of black spectral dogs have played a pivotal role in the Charles Walton story.

It was through the graveyard of St Swithin's, the church in Lower Quinton, that Charles Walton passed on his way to work that fateful morning. Locals say Walton's gravestone has been removed from church grounds to dissuade visitors.

The graveyard at St Swithin's. The gate Walton regularly walked through on his way to and from the fields can be seen in the background.

Fabian's prime suspect, John Alfred Potter, had a drink at the local pub, the College Arms, the morning of the murder.

Charles Walton's cottage stands opposite the church. It looks very much as it did back in Walton's day.

A crime scene photograph showing Walton's body, as it was found by Potter, Harold Beasley, and Walton's niece, Edith.

An undated photograph of Charles Walton.

Behind Walton's cottage stands a house with this curious weathervane. It is somewhat fitting, considering the spectre of witchcraft that has firmly attached itself to the Walton killing.

A section of the Rollright Stones, which feature prominently in the Walton murder. Some accounts claim Walton was killed in the centre of the ancient stone circle, which is 12 miles away from the actual murder site.

An overhead shot of modern-day Lower Quinton. The arrow points to the corner of the field where, according to Fabian, Walton's body was found. The circle shows the location of Walton's cottage, while the square marks the College Arms.

7

Suspicions Abound

On the day of the murder, John Lawrence Messer was delivering bread for Allan Valender. At 1.45 p.m. that afternoon, driving his bread van toward Lower Quinton, he saw on the outskirts of the village two Italian prisoners of war. It was not uncommon to see captured Italians roaming freely about the area. They generally caused no trouble and kept to themselves. The two Messer saw were standing on the left side of the road on a grass verge, alongside an old farming shed with an iron corrugated roof. He knew they were Italians because of their dark skin colour. One of them, he observed, was wearing a forage cap and chocolate-coloured battledress, and seemed very focussed on rubbing his hands clean with a dirty rag. As Messer drove past, the Italians seemed to avoid his gaze on purpose. The one rubbing his hands 'had an expression on his face as if he did not want to be seen'. Not until Messer's van was further down the road did he see, in the side mirror, the Italians watching him drive away. He rounded a bend and stopped at his next delivery. As he unloaded bread from the back of his van, he looked back down the road; the Italians were out of sight. Although the one had been doing nothing more than cleaning his hands, something about the incident struck Messer as 'suspicious'. He learned of Charles Walton's murder the next day.

Forty-five minutes after Messer saw the two Italians on the roadside, a farm labourer named Edward Hopkins was working a field near the POW camp in Long Marston when he saw an Italian approaching from the direction of Lower Quinton on the opposite side of a nearby brook. 'He was,' in Hopkins' words, 'walking fast, much faster than normal people walk – in fact it was a tremendous pace.' The prisoner seemed distracted, lost in his own thoughts, only to appear startled when he noticed Hopkins watching him. 'Afternoon,' the prisoner said, hurrying on his way. Hopkins returned the greeting and watched the Italian enter the main gates of the camp.

In questioning residents of Lower Quinton and the surrounding area, Fabian and Webb took statements from numerous individuals, including school children, who saw Italian prisoners strolling about the village on the day Walton died. It fell on Detective-Sergeant Saunders, the fluent Italian speaker dispatched by Scotland Yard's Special Branch to assist in the investigation, to pursue any leads at the Italian prison camp. Saunders arrived in Stratford-upon-Avon on the night of 16 February. He immediately set about reading statements already taken by officers of the Warwickshire Constabulary, in addition to Fabian and Webb. The villagers seemed to take a rather nonchalant view of captured enemy combatants wandering about the place. It was not uncommon to see Italian prisoners in the local post office, purchasing cigarettes and sweets. In reviewing the statements, it was interesting to note that only Hopkins reported seeing an Italian in the fields, while all other residents saw prisoners strolling along the main road between Upper and Lower Quinton, or in the villages themselves. Hopkins even mentioned there was no proper footpath along the route he saw the Italian taking. Even though it was some 2 miles from the scene of the crime, it was deemed worthy of further investigation.

Officers sent to the area found footprints along the route and took a plaster cast of one. It would prove to be of little evidentiary value. 'The characteristics shown by the cast were similar to many of the boots worn by Italian prisoners-of-war,' Fabian would write in his official report, 'all their boots being repaired to a standard pattern and in accordance with regulations.' Saunders spent two weeks at the camp, interviewing inmates and prison officials. Villagers who reported seeing Italians walking about the area on the day of the crime were brought in and asked to point the inmates out of a line-up. No one could positively identify the Italians they saw on the day in question. Even Messer, who – in his statement to police – described down to the man's dental work the Italian he saw cleaning his hands at the side of the road, was unable to make a positive identification. Subsequently, Fabian dismissed Messer's story as fabrication. Saunders, however, was able to ascertain who among the inmates had wandered into the village that day. The Italians were cooperative, even courteous, during interrogation. What soon emerged was evidence of a camp system in which security was lackadaisical at best, allowing inmates to come and go as they pleased. 'The conditions prevailing at Long Marston Camp,' Fabian wrote in his report, 'are such that it would be impossible, with certainty, to say who was in or out of the camp at any particular time.'

The prisoners said they often left the camp to purchase goods in Upper and Lower Quinton. Barracks were searched and uniforms examined for trace evidence of blood. As police worked their way through one hut, searching lockers and stripping beds, they noticed an Italian prisoner frantically reaching for something under his bunk. When confronted, the inmate – a man named Annunzio Duchetta – showed officers several wire snares used for poaching rabbits. Scared he might get in trouble for poaching, Duchetta confessed he sometimes sold captured game to local villagers for a little extra spending money. Such was Duchetta's level of concern for a relatively minor crime that Fabian did not consider him a suspect. It would turn out to be the only evidence of bloodshed investigators stumbled across at the camp. In all, sixty-eight statements were taken from inmates at the camp – and more than 1,100 were subjected to personal searches. As Fabian wrote to his superiors back in London:

> From enquiries I have made in this matter, I have been unable to establish that any of these Italians have ever resorted to violence during their stay at Long Marston and cannot find one authentic case of any of them even being discourteous to local villagers. The result of all these intensive enquiries into the movements of Italians on the 14th February 1945 does not reveal any evidence which could connect them with the murder.

Fabian's attention circled back once more to Alfred Potter. He had made every effort, save one, to account for the man's whereabouts on the day of the murder, but the mystery of Potter's movements between noon and 1 p.m. continued to nettle. Even while pursuing the Italian angle, Fabian had continued probing into Potter's background, seeking out those who had worked for him at one time or another. In doing so, he met yet another man who – like George Purnell and Walton – had trouble with Potter when it came to wages. William Dyde had worked five years under Potter's employ until November 1944, when he quit. Dyde told Fabian he would often work overtime, particularly at harvest time, but had trouble collecting his extra pay. He would sometimes go three weeks without receiving his wages. At times, he said, it seemed as if Potter was short of money. Like Purnell, Dyde said Potter was fond of his drink and an unpleasant personality.

Potter obviously had money issues of some sort and was short-changing employees to make up for his financial woes. Money, Fabian still believed, lay at the heart of the crime. On 27 February, he sent a Metropolitan Police Telegram to Inspector Digby of Scotland Yard's CID, asking him to run a background check on Potter's finances. He also asked that an additional round of queries be made with fences, pawnbrokers, and jewellers to see if Walton's missing watch had shown up. In London, Digby checked with Stubbs and Bradsheet, two providers of credit information on businesses, and reported back to Fabian via telegram the following day. There were no debts recorded against Alfred John Potter or his father's company, L.L. Potter & Company. A description of Walton's watch was again being circulated amongst those who operated – legally or otherwise – in the jewellery trade. Also, on Fabian's orders, a request for records pertaining to Potter's business had been made with the wages branch of the Ministry of Agriculture and Fisheries. Fabian wanted a complete financial picture of Potter and his operation.

Fabian was running out of options. The canvassing of Lower Quinton and the surrounding district failed to turn up anything of particular value. It never ceased to amaze Fabian that in an area where everyone seemed to know one another, no one knew anything about the killing. On 16 March, he received a brief report from James M. Webster at the West Midland Forensic Science Laboratory pertaining to the work clothes Fabian had confiscated from Potter:

Dear Sir,
I have the honour to report that I examined the articles submitted on the 24th February and labelled as belonging to Potter. I could

find nothing of evidential value upon these garments. There were two areas upon the breeches, which gave presumptive tests for blood, but they had been so well cleaned that it was impossible to say whether or not this blood had been human or not.

On one hand, it could be said this was circumstantial evidence against Potter; on the other, would it not be normal for a farmer to wash his breeches clean of animal blood? Why, however, was there trace amount of blood only on the knees of the breeches? Did Potter kill Walton and then, while kneeling down to go through the dead man's clothing, get blood on the knees? During those forty minutes that remained unaccounted for, did Potter hurry back to the farm and frantically scrub his breeches clean? Again, a farmer cleaning his work clothes in and of itself was not suspicious, but the soiled area of the breeches had been scrubbed inordinately clean – cleaner than the rest of the garments; cleaned so well forensics couldn't even establish the type of blood present. Why was it necessary to clean them to such an excessive degree? Surely, he would dirty them again the next time he worked.

It was time, Fabian decided, to question Lilian Potter. There was, of course, the chance her husband had already coached her on what to say – but so be it. The woman's demeanour, the details she provided, would tell Fabian something. On the morning of 17 March, Fabian and Webb returned to The Firs. They gave Lilian Potter no prior warning. When they knocked on the door, she seemed nonplussed to see them. Alfred, she said, was in the fields. She could send a farmhand to go and fetch him. Fabian smiled and said that wouldn't be necessary. It was her they wanted to see. She led them into the kitchen, where they had first questioned her husband, and boiled some water for tea.

'You knew Walton,' said Fabian. It was more a statement than a question.

'He used to call at the house occasionally for his money on a Saturday,' she said, taking a seat at the table. 'I would sometimes give him a glass of cider. I never conversed with him. I don't know what time he used to start work in the mornings.'

'Did you help in the business?'

Lilian replied:

I used to make up the wage sheets for the farm on every Friday.
I would ask my husband how much to put down for Mr Walton
and he would tell me the amount. I don't know how much work
Mr Walton did, but I do know that he didn't work on Saturdays or
if the weather was bad.

'Walk us through Wednesday, 14 February. Do you remember what
you did?'
She said:

I remember, during the morning, I prepared breakfast for Miss Savory
and Mrs Wilson, the ambulance workers who are billeted at my
house, at about 8.30 a.m. I think my husband had breakfast at about
half past nine to ten and then left the house to go about his work.
I then got on with my household duties. I did not see Mr Walton that
morning. Round about eleven o'clock my husband came to the house
to fetch some implements to castrate some calves for Mr Stanley.
He was only in the house a few minutes. I did not leave the house
that morning.

She paused and looked at Fabian as if for confirmation she was doing
okay. He encouraged her to continue and asked her about that afternoon:

At some time after half-past twelve – it could not have been many
minutes after – my husband came into the kitchen and sat reading
the paper for a few minutes. He said, 'How long will dinner be?'
and I told him it wouldn't be long. He said, 'I've got to go and help
"Happy" to pulp some mangolds.' And then he left the house.

'And you're sure of the time?' Fabian asked.
Lilian answered:

Yes. When my husband came into the house I switched the wireless
on to see if my clock was right. The 'Workers' Playtime' programme
was on. I am quite sure it was twenty to one by my clock when my
husband left the house. I was studying the time for dinner. At about
five past one, my husband came in for his dinner. I was listening to
the news on the wireless. We sat and had our dinner together.

'What did you have?' asked Fabian, glancing up from his notebook.

'I don't remember,' Lilian said, not thinking much of the question:

After we had finished, I made a cup of tea, and whilst we were having it, the baker's roundsman from Valender's came to deliver the bread. He stayed and had a cup of tea. I am not sure what time the baker's roundsman came or left, but it was between half past one and two.

She paused as Fabian made note of something she said. He offered her a quick smile and urged her to continue:

At ten past or a quarter past two, my husband left the house. He came back shortly afterwards and telephoned to Russell's about a heifer he had in a ditch. He went out again immediately in our car and returned with the car in about a quarter of an hour. After that, I saw him ride past on Russell's tractor. I don't know what time this was.

'So, you were outside the house at this point?' asked Fabian.

'Directly after dinner, I started to trim a japonica tree near my front door,' Lilian said. 'That is how I came to see my husband on the tractor.'

'And when did you see your husband next?'

'I did not see my husband again until about four o'clock,' she said. 'I cannot be sure of the time. He came in for the milk buckets. He only stayed a few minutes. My husband next came in at about six o'clock to his tea.'

'Right,' said Fabian, as if finally getting to some long-awaited point, 'what happened that evening?'

Lilian said she and her husband were having their tea when, at about 6.20 p.m., there was a knock on the door. Lilian answered and found Edith Walton standing on the doorstep with Harry Beasley. Edith asked if Mr Potter was home and said she was worried, as her uncle had never returned from work. She feared something had happened to him. Alfred came to the door and, expressing similar concern, offered to take Edith and Beasley to the field where Walton had been working that day.

Lilian said:

They crossed the orchard by the side of the churchyard, and I saw them go towards Meon Hill. I then went to shut the fowls up and, as I was crossing the lawn, Miss Savory pushed her window up and said, 'Shall I come with you to shut up the fowls?' I told her that the hedge cutter hadn't come home and after a few minutes she came out and we decided to follow the others to see if we could help. Miss Savory and I crossed some fields towards Meon Hill, when I heard a shout. I said, 'That sounds like Alf's voice.' Soon after, we saw Mr Beasley and Miss Walton coming back. Miss Walton was crying. Mr Beasley said, 'He's dead.' I said, 'Where's Alf?' and he replied, 'He's got to stay there until I get back.' We all four walked back together to the field where the caravan is. We there met Mrs Nicholls and Mrs Beasley.

'And then what did you do?' asked Fabian.
She said:

I then waited in the road in case Mr Lomasney came and wanted to know where to go. I waited for some time and then returned to the house. I told them what I had heard and I then waited in the kitchen until about half past nine when my husband came home. Mr Stanley came in at about the same time. I don't know if he was with my husband. My husband said, 'The police think it's murder.' He told me that a slashing hook was stuck into Mr Walton's neck. As far as I can remember, that was all my husband said. Mr Stanley and my husband discussed how horrible it was.

Lilian Potter, her voice breaking, pulled a handkerchief from her purse and dabbed her eyes.
'My husband,' she said, struggling to maintain her composure, 'looked bad and he said the sight had made him feel sick.'
Fabian gave her a minute to recover before gently asking her what happened next.
She said:

Just after 9.30 p.m., I went with my husband in our car to Chipping Campden. I went to my mother's house, and he went to the Lygon

Arms Public House. We only stayed a few minutes and then came straight back. We got home at about a quarter past ten. Three policemen came and conversed with my husband about the murder. They left after eleven o'clock. We then went straight to bed. We have both been very upset about this affair due to the fact that it happened on our land. Neither of us slept very well the first night or so after the murder.

'Did your husband tell you he touched anything at the crime scene?'

'I remember that on the day after the murder, my husband mentioned to PC Lomasney that he – my husband – had touched the slashing hook when he found the body,' Lilian said, her voice once more trembling with emotion.

'What did he say about it?'

'He told PC Lomasney that Mr Beasley had asked him to make sure that Mr Walton was dead, and that it was then that he touched the slashing hook.'

'The breeches your husband wears about the farm, does he wash them often?' Fabian asked.

'I am sure that my husband has never cleaned his breeches,' she said. 'I mean, the ones the police took from him.'

This struck Fabian, for someone had certainly subjected the breeches to a thorough cleaning.

'You've been quite specific with the times in your statement,' Fabian said, changing course. 'You're confident the times are correct?'

'I am sure that my husband came in at a few minutes after half past twelve on the 14th February and went out to pulp mangolds at twenty to one,' she said. 'I am also sure he came into dinner at five past one. I cannot be sure of other times on that day.'

Fabian finished his tea and closed his notebook. It now seemed 'perfectly obvious' to Fabian that Potter had briefed his wife well on what times to tell police he was in and out of the house. Under the circumstances, it was hardly surprising.

'Thank you for your time, Mrs Potter,' he said. 'We'll show ourselves out.'

Fabian remained silent until he and Webb got back in their car. He felt he was running in circles, merely repeating the same questions over and over again with nothing to show for his efforts. It seemed almost unfathomable that here, amongst the thatched-roofs and winding lanes of the English countryside, a crime so brutal could possibly go unsolved. The investigation had now been ongoing for a month and yet he had failed to establish any clear motive. What he had against Potter hardly amounted to circumstantial evidence. The discrepancies in Potter's statements did not justify an arrest. Lilian Potter's statement, which further fuelled Fabian's suspicions, gave him nothing concrete to act on. While Webb drove, Fabian reviewed his notes.

'It's remarkable,' he said, 'that whilst Mrs Potter is so certain of the exact times her husband came and went round about dinner time that day, she cannot recall what they had for dinner or be sure of any other times during the day.'

Webb nodded. Fabian stared out the car window, brooding. Something else in the woman's statement didn't ring true. She said the day after the murder, her husband mentioned to PC Lomasney that he touched the slashing hook after Beasley told him to make sure Walton was dead. Lomasney, however, had told Fabian that Potter only mentioned touching the implement on the evening of 20 February, after Lomasney brought up the subject of fingerprints. Furthermore, Beasley had already told Fabian that he asked Potter to do no such thing. Fabian rubbed a hand across his tired eyes. Why was it proving so hard to get at the truth? Whatever the story, Potter remained Fabian's prime suspect.

Fabian later wrote in his case report:

Every effort has been made to check Potter's movements that morning. Other than his wife, who says he returned to the house at 'sometime after half-past twelve,' nobody can say they saw him from about 12 noon until 12.40 p.m. when Batchelor, the cowman, says he came to the mixing house and helped him to pulp some mangolds. Batchelor fixes the time by the fact that he and Potter went to look at the church clock and it was then 1 p.m. Potter himself says that he helped Batchelor for about five minutes before looking at the church clock and it therefore appears more than likely that it was later than 12.40 p.m. when Batchelor first saw Potter.

Then, Fabian stated the crux of the matter:

> However, the fact remains that whatever Potter did between
> 12 noon and 1 p.m. he would have had ample time to have
> committed the murder for, by his own admission, he was in an
> adjoining field at 12.20 p.m.

✳

Potter testified at the continuation of the coroner's inquest on
Tuesday, 20 March. When Potter took the stand, the coroner
explained that as he, Potter, was the last one to see Walton alive, the
questioning to follow would be quite detailed. Potter stated his name
and occupation for the record before the coroner launched into his
examination.

'Do you know whether Walton carried any money about with him?'

'I don't,' Potter said.

'Have you seen the watch he owned?'

'Only when I asked him the time.'

'Have you seen the chain?' the coroner asked.

'No, sir.'

'Did you see him early that morning?'

'No, sir,' said Potter, 'not before he began work. I saw someone at
about 12.30, but I would not say it was him.'

When asked to elaborate on his activities the day of the murder,
Potter told the story he had by now repeated several times to investigators. He told the inquest he spent several minutes in the College
Arms and left at noon. He walked to Joseph Stanley's farm and spent
ten minutes watching Stanley work on his tractor. Potter then went
back to his own farm to drop off some tools before making his way
to the fields to check on his sheep and calves. While feeding a bale
of hay to some cattle, he saw a man he thought was Walton at a distance of 500 yards working in the neighbouring field.

'I am not sure it was him,' Potter said, 'but I saw someone in his
shirtsleeves.'

'At the time,' the coroner interjected, 'you thought it was him?'

'That's right, sir,' Potter replied.

'Was he using any tools?'

'Well,' said Potter with a shrug, 'I can't say; I never saw him move.
I just thought at the time it was him, and went on.'

Potter continued to detail the remainder of his day. He said Edith Walton and Harry Beasley knocked on his door at 6.15 p.m. that evening, shortly after tea. Upon hearing Walton had not yet returned home, and knowing the old man was always back in his cottage by 4 p.m., he feared something had happened. He led Edith and Beasley to the field where Walton had been working and discovered the body.

'Did you touch him at all?' the coroner asked.

'No, sir,' Potter replied.

'You could see he was seriously hurt?'

'I could, sir.'

'You never interfered with the body?'

'Well, sir, Mr Beasley said I had better make sure Walton was dead, so I went back and caught hold of the trouncing hook. That was all I touched.'

'You satisfied yourself he was dead?'

'It was the first time I had seen a dead body.'

'You couldn't help further in any way?' the coroner asked.

'I'm afraid not,' Potter said. 'I wish I could.'

Asked if he got along well with the victim, Potter said he 'never had a row with any man'. Walton could be relied upon to get his work done. 'I trusted him,' Potter said.

Sitting in the front and listening to the testimony, Fabian noticed a discrepancy in Potter's version of events. He informed the coroner that when first interviewed by himself and Webb on 17 February, Potter said he went straight to get the heifer out of the ditch after feeding his livestock in the fields. Now, he seemed to have reversed the order of those two events.

'I wonder,' Fabian said, 'which is right.'

The coroner turned to Potter and offered a reassuring smile to a witness who now seemed nervous.

'I don't want to unduly press you,' the coroner said, 'but which is correct?'

'What I have said now,' Potter replied without hesitation.

'Were you very disturbed?'

'I was very cut up,' Potter said, nodding.

There was no one Potter said, under continued questioning, with whom Walton had any sort of disagreement. The day of the murder he saw nothing that would have aroused any suspicion. He did see several soldiers in the village and wandering around Meon Hill, but such activity during wartime had become part of the norm. Asked if there was anything in his field that might attract someone, Potter could think of nothing more than rabbits. And, with that, the farmer was excused.

Fabian watched Potter leave.

8

Beyond the Case Files

Tales of the occult, witchcraft, and Satan worshipping attached themselves to the Lower Quinton murder early on. Although Fabian seems to pay these stories little heed in the official case file, his belief in such things seems to fluctuate. In his book *London After Dark*, he writes:

> The practice of Black Magic – of diabolical religious rites in the heart of London – is spreading steadily. There is more active Satan-worship today than ever since the Dark Ages, when witches were publicly burned upon Tower Hill.

As a police officer, prior to the Lower Quinton murder, he took an interest in the occult and witchcraft, as he believed it 'posed a menace to society'. In *The Anatomy of Crime*, Fabian details several witchcraft-related cases that came to the attention of Scotland Yard. In one, a man – 'obsessed with witchcraft and abnormal violence' – took a carving knife and stabbed his neighbour's 12-year-old child to death. He avoided justice by taking his own life. Indeed, witchcraft, Fabian argued, endangered the moral fabric of society:

> Witchcraft can break up marriages. I know of wives who objected, with reason, to their husbands going off for nude frolics with other women … Witchcraft, in my opinion, is little more than a glorified excuse for men and women to grovel in their bases and foulest animal urges in an aura of pseudo-respectability.

By the mid-1930s, police claimed there were four practising 'occult magic circles' in London. It was believed these fraternities relied upon a series of four books, known as *Magick*, which detailed the proper ways to conduct 'the celebration of masses, magical litanies, other rites of wizardry, and ceremonial blood sacrifices upon an altar'. To those of a skeptical nature, it may all sound ridiculous, yet Fabian believed real danger attached itself to such activities. Often times, membership to these occults was found in the well-to-do. One 'circle' met in a well-furnished studio in Chelsea, while another occupied an entire house in Lancaster Gate. At these places, practitioners of black magic would gather and perform their ritualistic ceremonies. The gatherers at Chelsea, known as the Order of St Bridget, supposedly stripped naked, assumed the shape of the cross with arms outstretched, and were whipped by other worshippers – '"Inquisitors" dressed in monks' cowls, until they "confess".'

The majority of people who attended black masses, wrote Fabian, did so out of simple curiosity. It was to them, initially, a unique form of entertainment – yet behind the novelty, lurked a real threat. 'They do not realise – until it is too late – that in these temples of Satan, brain-stealing herbal incenses and hypnotic devices are mercilessly used – until the man or girl who came just to stare and giggle may find themselves trapped.' Fabian cites a case on file with Scotland Yard relating to a 21-year-old woman – a promising concert singer – who, with her mother, attended a lecture on Satanism. The talk was administered by the 'High Priestess' of a local cult, who took a liking to the young woman and began spending time with her. One day, the young woman left her house and failed to return. Her frantic parents alerted Scotland Yard. When she was found some months later, it was discovered 'the girl had been hypnotised and exposed to occult obscenities so persistently that she was almost insane. Her own pet dog ran howling in fear from her. It took two years to restore her mind.' No one was ever prosecuted in connection with the case, for the girl could not provide the names of her tormentors. No witnesses ever stepped forward. The cult, it seems, had wiped her memory clean of specific details.

While Fabian's words carry a certain hyperbole, book four of *Magick* carries a similar warning about such things:

The student, if he attains any success in the following practices, will find himself confronted by things (ideas or beings) too glorious or too dreadful to be described. It is essential that he remain the master of all that he beholds, hears or conceives; otherwise he will be the slave of illusion and the prey of madness.

The author of these words was none other than Aleister Crowley, also known as 'The Beast' and 'The Most Wickedest Man in the World'. In a tenuous connection, Crowley's name would later surface in the Lower Quinton affair. Despite his belief in the dangers of witchcraft, Fabian dismissed it as nothing more than a crude cult – one that did not shy away from making easy money. Like all cults, witchcraft targeted people who could easily be exploited, Fabian theorised, with lonely middle-aged men and women with personal problems being particular favourites. If those targeted were individuals with wealth who owned large houses where covens could congregate to drink blood, flog one another, and worship Pagan symbols, then all the more better.

Out of curiosity, Fabian decided to attend a black mass to see for himself what these fiends got up to. It was not difficult to find such events in the city, he wrote in his memoirs. He knew of a man in West London who ran a temple off the Bayswater Road. All one had to do was call and reserve a seat for the evening's dark festivities, which Fabian did under an assumed name.

On the night in question, Fabian arrived at the temple – actually a 'house converted into flatlets' – and, having his reservation confirmed at the door, was told to make his way down to the cellar. He descended a dimly lit staircase and, upon reaching the cellar, was directed through a hole in the wall that passed into the cellar of the house next door. From there, he was ushered up another staircase to a door lined in black felt. 'This,' wrote Fabian, 'is the entrance to the Temple of Satanism. Inside, the walls and ceiling are covered with magic symbols. Oil lamps, burning a dark green fat, give off a hideous smell, their purpose being, I suspect, to blanket the odour of the chloroform or ether with which the room is sprayed.'

Against the far wall, beneath an upside down crucifix, was a traditional church altar adorned in black candles that cast flickering shadows on the ceiling. Off to one side of the altar, a group of men and women in open robes rubbed their bodies against an 'obscenely fashioned' five-foot tall statue of an African fertility god. Somewhere a clock struck midnight, and the mass got under way 'with chants and responses intoned in Latin':

> When the communion wafers have been blasphemed and soiled the nauseating fragments are hidden in lockets or are mixed with the wax in little wax images, empowering the images to invoke curses upon enemies. The success with which respectable, ordinary men and women are duped into participating in these outlandish capers is clearly complete. They look ridiculous. And very pathetic.

Although Fabian thought the whole thing to be rubbish, he didn't dismiss the dangers he believed were inherent in such behaviour and beliefs. Witchcraft, he asserted, 'excited terror and brought out the worst in people'. Is this what happened in Lower Quinton? Many accounts detailing Walton's murder claim that it is. Supposed 'witnesses' would step forward years after the killing, proclaiming the Lower Quinton murder was the result of a black magic ritual and the work of a coven. That people made such assertions is perhaps not surprising when one considers the Cotswolds and Warwickshire are heavily steeped in stories of witchcraft, ghosts, and other dark happenings. In 1897, journalist George Morley surveyed the folk-customs and superstitions of Shakespeare Country and concluded many in the region held onto beliefs long discarded by city dwellers. He wrote:

> This is the more remarkable bearing the fact in mind that Warwickshire is the central county of England, open to all the influences of modern civilisation, and in many seasons of the year simply overrun with visitors, who may be supposed to bring with them the new ideas, the new fancies, and the new language of a new people.

He traced the belief in witches and the supernatural back to Warwickshire's earliest days, when dark, ancient woods lent the county a haunted atmosphere. The wind, whistling through branches, the skeletal shadows cast by sun and moonlight, and the eerie cries of animals unseen played upon the fertile imaginations of the 'simple' woodlanders who made the area their home. Successive generations passed down their beliefs in late-night stories and cautionary tales. Not all superstitions were of the evil variety; indeed, some were quaint in nature and reflected the simplicity of country life. The melodic calling of a magpie could predict the fortunes of a nearby listener:

> One magpie means sorrow; two mirth;
> Three a wedding; four a birth.

But in one area of Warwickshire, the Vale of the Red Horse, beliefs in witches and dark magic were rampant. The area, situated beneath the escarpment of Edgehill, is named for the large horse-shaped figure that once appeared etched in the hill's red clay soil. The first mention of the horse appears in a 1606 cartography report on the region. Its origin unknown, it was of considerable size, measuring 34 feet from croup to chest, 16 feet from shoulder to ground with a 12-foot-long foreleg, an eye more than a foot in diameter, and an 18-foot-long tail. Today, the horse no longer exists, as 'successive generations of local villagers and landowners' have allowed vegetation to reclaim the site. In old Europe it was believed witches stole horses at night and rode them hard to their nocturnal covens, returning them before sunrise. The 1875 murder of a supposed witch in Long Compton, according to Morley, sent the country folk in the Vale of the Red Horse into a near frenzy. 'All the little, lonely villages, clustering there in silence and suspicion,' the journalist wrote, 'were bitten by the craze for witch finding. Whether Long Compton started the cry or not cannot be well determined, but it passed mysteriously from village to village and made a very sad time for ancient dames.'

Paranoia and suspicion spread, shrouding the Vale like an all-encompassing mist. Residents in the village of Tysoe believed an ancient woman who lived among them was a practitioner of black magic. The rumour gained such momentum that villagers from nearby Brailes descended on Tysoe, seized the woman, and punctured her hand with a corking pin in an attempt to bleed away her powers. To a detective of Fabian's calibre and experience, such stories may have sounded quaint, the product of overwrought imaginations and midnight fairytales. In his memoirs, however, he would play up the superstition angle. Writing of the villagers in Lower Quinton, he noted, many 'will not pass from Bidford down Hillborough-lane for fear of a headless horseman and a ghostly woman in white'. In his 1897 article, Morley references not a headless horseman, but a 'night coach' – an apparition 'peculiar in woody districts' – and encountered by many who claimed to have seen the ghostly vision on moonlit nights, flickering like a mirage on deserted hills and lanes outside the village of Mickleton, near Lower Quinton. Witnesses described the coach as an old, mid-eighteenth century family carriage drawn by six horses the shade of midnight. It would traverse the Warwickshire hills on its nocturnal run and cross over into Gloucestershire, navigating the steep country with a speed that would be impossible for any earthbound carriage, horse, or coachman to achieve.

In his 1929 book *Folk Lore, Old Customs and Superstitions in Shakespeare Land*, J. Harvey Bloom – an English clergyman and antiquary fascinated by local legends – spoke with villagers who lived in the shadow of Meon Hill. Many he interviewed said they had no doubt the region was a lively centre of witchcraft. Witches, however, were not the only thing villagers believed plagued the bucolic landscape:

> Among the villages of the plain below the hill are many old folk living to tell those they can trust creepy stories of the Hell-hounds, Night-hounds, or Hooter, as they are variously named, that in phantom wise, with hounds and horn, pursue phantom foxes along the hill-tops at midnight. Many are the legends to account for uncouth sounds at night, which certainly do occur. One story is told of a local huntsman who would not desist from his favourite sport even on the Sabbath. On one Sunday judgement fell upon the ungodly crew; huntsmen, horses and hounds fell into a chasm that opened in the hill and were never seen again, though they still in ghostly wise hunt at midnight.

One ghostly story that would firmly attach itself to the Lower Quinton episode involved a boy named, coincidentally, Charles Walton. According to legend, as detailed in Bloom's book, the boy had spent a day working the fields around Meon Hill. As the sun began to set one evening in 1885, the boy headed for home. A solitary figure, he walked the darkening lane and watched the ground mist gather in the fields on either side. Something materialised in the gloom. The young boy watched in dread as a large, black dog, its eyes glowing red, emerged from the swirling dusk. The animal sat along the roadside and followed the boy with its gaze. Young Walton forced himself to look away and hurried for the safety and comfort of home.

Believed to be guardians of the underworld, black dogs have long been a part of British folklore. Nearly every county in England has a story centred on this phantom beast, which is generally associated with witchcraft and Satanism. During the 1566 Chelmsford Witch Trials in Essex, 18-year-old Joan Waterhouse stood accused of summoning a black dog 'with a short tail, the face of an ape, a pair of horns on his head and a silver whistle around his neck' to wreak havoc in the village. Joan was spared the gallows after she testified against her mother, Agnes, claiming the elder woman relied on a feline spirit named Satan to do her will. Agnes Waterhouse became the first woman to be hanged in England for witchcraft when she went to the gallows on 24 July 1566. The phantom canines are believed to be omens of death. This is particularly so with 'Black Shuck', the most infamous of England's ghostly hounds. Described by those who have supposedly seen him as being equal in size to a calf and possessing eyes of fiery red or glowing green, 'Shuck' supposedly haunts 'graveyards, lonely country roads, misty marshes and the hills around villages'. The beast's name is derived from the word 'succa', Anglo-Saxon for 'demon'. In recent times, it has been claimed by motorists that 'Shuck' has run in front of their cars, only to vanish when the car passes through him.

It is said, in the most infamous tale of its kind, that a black dog ransacked St Mary's Church, Bungay, Suffolk, during a violent storm in 1577. It was 4 August – a Sunday – and congregants had gathered for the morning service. Outside, rain began to fall and soon turned torrential, as thunder rolled across a blackened sky. 'The church,' according to one contemporary account, 'did as it were quake and stagger, which struck into the hearts of those that were present such a sore and sudden fear, that they were robbed in a manner of their right wits'. A strong wind thrashed the building and blew open the church doors. Standing on the rain-battered threshold, much to the horror of the parishioners, was a hulking black beast with fiery eyes and drooling snout. The horrible vision, so the witness account goes, 'moved such admiration in the minds of the assembly, that they thought Doomday had already come'. The account continues:

This Black Dog, or the devil in such a likeness (God he Knoweth all who worketh all) running all along down the body of the church with great swiftness, and incredible haste, among the people in a visible form and shape, passed between two persons as they were kneeling on their knees, and occupied in prayer as it seems, wrung the necks of them both at one instant clean backward, insomuch that even at the moment where they kneeled they strangely died.

The dog continued its rampage through the church, mauling one man in the back and leaving him 'as shrunken as a piece of leather scorched in hot fire'. Witnessing the mayhem, the church rector, 'being partaker of the people's perplexity,' demanded the terrified parishioners to pray. This they did, as the dog bounded from the building. In the aftermath, the incident was deemed 'a wonderful example of God's wrath, no doubt to terrify us, that we might fear Him for His justice, or pulling back our footsteps from the paths of sin, to love Him for His mercy'. The author of this account, Abraham Fleming, knowing the report 'to some will seem absurd' offered the following:

As testimonies and witnesses of the force which rested in this strange shaped thing, there are remaining in the stones of the Church, and likewise in the Church door, which are marvelously reten and torn, the marks as it were of his claws or talons.

The incident would soon be immortalised in a local verse:

All down the church in midst of fire, the hellish monster flew
And, passing onward to the quire, he many people slew.

Growing up in the country, young Walton had surely heard stories of this ghostly menace and knew a visit from such an apparition meant a loved one would soon die. The day after his sighting, he returned to the fields of Meon Hill to continue his harvesting. That night, as he again walked home alone, the hound took shape in the mist. The dog showed itself to Walton once more the following night. This time, however, a headless woman, smoky and transparent, walked alongside the boy's tormentor. The woman suddenly rushed past Walton and, just as quickly, vanished. The boy, terrified, ran home. The next day, his sister passed away unexpectedly. The origins of this story are not known – but it, too, became part of local lore and an apocryphal element of the Lower Quinton story. Many accounts of the Lower Quinton murder assume the Charles Walton in the black dog story is the same individual who wound up murdered in the shadow of Meon Hill. Those who make this assumption add to the storyline, claiming Walton's childhood haunting imbued him with powers of clairvoyance and that he went from being an outgoing, happy boy, to a reclusive, lonely old man. 'For the remainder of his 74 years,' states one source, 'Walton withdrew into himself. He worked for meagre wages, seldom drank in public, and was left alone by his neighbours.'

The question to ask is whether the Walton boy in the story was the same Walton who met his grisly fate at the end of a pitchfork? The answer is most likely no. Walton, according to British census records, had three older sisters: Mary Ann, Martha, and Harriett (a half-sister). For Walton, the murder victim, to be the same Walton featured in Bloom's tale of the ghostly hound and headless apparition means one of his sisters would have had to have died in 1885. Census records, however, show Mary Ann and Martha both married in 1891, while Harriett was still alive in 1901.

✳

Fabian writes about the Lower Quinton investigation in two volumes of memoirs. In one account, he half-heartedly suggests a possible witchcraft connection; in another, he claims outright the slaying was the result of a black magic ritual. If one moves beyond the official Scotland Yard case files and goes solely by Fabian's personal account, the investigation does take a slight supernatural bent. In both books, he details an encounter with what he gently suggests to the reader might be a spectral hound.

Walton's killing, he writes, was one of 'slaughterhouse horror'. Initially, wrote Fabian, he believed the case to be a straightforward homicide – but strange occurrences soon convinced him otherwise. One bleak afternoon, he made his way through the tombstones in the St Swithin's graveyard and emerged into the fields beyond the church. Beneath a cold, grey sky, he passed through hedge-bordered fields and made the ascent up Meon Hill. He raised the collar of his trench coat against the wind and lowered his head to prevent his hat from blowing off. Near the top, he paused and turned around. The villages of Upper and Lower Quinton looked bucolic in the near-distance, surrounded by fields and meandering lanes. Somewhere down there, in that quaint setting, lurked a killer, going about his normal daily routine and benefitting from the reluctance of country folk to open up to outsiders. The hill itself, however, struck Fabian as bleak and desolate. No sound from the villages reached the fields up here. As Fabian stood with his hands in his pockets, a black dog – 'a retriever' – appeared on a nearby stone wall that bisected the field. It sat and watched Fabian for a moment before jumping off the wall and trotting past him. Fabian paid the dog little attention. Several minutes later a young farm boy entered the field.

'Looking for your dog?' Fabian asked him.

'What dog?' the boy replied.

'A black dog ...'

Fabian never finished his sentence. Upon hearing the detective utter the words 'black dog,' the boy – with a look of sheer panic on his face – turned and fled down the hill in the direction from which he'd been walking. According to Fabian, word soon spread through Lower Quinton that he had seen 'The Ghost'. Fabian writes that he was skeptical when talk first turned to witchcraft and black magic. That afternoon, a police car on routine patrol on the outskirts of the village struck and killed a black dog that darted into the lane. There were, Fabian writes in his memoirs, murmurings around Lower Quinton of a greater evil at play. The next day, according to Fabian, another heifer was found dead in a ditch on Meon Hill. It was not until a dead black dog was supposedly found strung up from a bush near the spot where Walton died that Fabian, as he would later write with dramatic flair, 'realised for certain we were up against witch-craft'. Fabian writes in his memoirs that he believed the residents of Lower Quinton were hiding something from him – and this bears out in the official case files. Yet he strays from what's recorded in police files by asserting that villagers, when questioned, hinted that something supernatural was to blame for the Walton tragedy:

We made our investigation in the village from door to door. There were lowered eyes, reluctance to speak except of talk of bad crops – a heifer that died in a ditch. But what had that to do with Charles Walton? Nobody would say.

In the case files, there are no statements that allude to bad crops or dead dogs hanging from bushes. The dead heifer is mentioned, but only because Potter told police one of his cows had drowned in a ditch and he needed the help of another farmer to remove it. No one ever insinuated that a link existed between the dead animal and some evil spell. Is it possible Fabian heard such talk not on the record, but as casual banter one evening while sipping a pint in the College Arms? Or was Fabian merely exercising a little creative license with his telling of the story, capitalising on the myths and legends that were already cropping up around the crime? It could possibly be a combination of both. In *Fabian of the Yard*, he writes that when villagers learned he had seen a black dog on Meon Hill, the whole atmosphere in Lower Quinton changed:

When Albert Webb and I walked into the village pub that evening, silence fell like a physical blow. Cottage doors were shut in our faces, and even the most innocent witnesses seemed unable to meet our eyes. Some became ill after we spoke to them.

This again deviates from the Scotland Yard files and is undoubtedly an exaggeration of what really occurred – however, it shouldn't be dismissed as completely out of hand. After all, it is quite possible some villagers refused to speak with a stranger from London. And some, while conversing over drinks, might be prone to watch what they say knowing the police are listening. On one occasion, Fabian writes, he and Webb knocked on a door that was answered by an elderly gentleman. 'I'm inquiring about the late Charles Walton—' Fabian said, but was unable to finish his sentence. 'He's been dead and buried a month now,' the old man said with little patience. 'What are you worrying about?' The door was promptly slammed in Fabian's face.

9

THE SPECTRE OF WITCHCRAFT

In the two official case reports Fabian filed in connection with the Walton murder, he makes no mention of witchcraft. He does, however, allude to something sinister behind the scenes:

> The natives of Upper and Lower Quinton and the surrounding district are of a secretive disposition and they do not take easily to strangers. Therefore, I have borne in mind the possibility of there being some local history attached to the murdered man or his neighbours which we have not yet touched upon and which may have a direct bearing upon the murder.

In his first volume of memoirs, *Fabian of the Yard*, published eight years after the crime, Fabian is more blunt in his assessment. In his introduction to the Walton murder, he writes:

> Anybody can become a witch. All you have to do is to recite an ancient spell that will conjure up the devil. You then dip a quill pen in blood from your veins and sign an agreement selling him your soul. He gives you a silver coin token, and leaves you with a cat, a bird and a black dog, which will act as your fiendish servant and obey your commands. Such is the ritual of black witchery, and you should be warned that it is an offence under the Witchcraft Act of 1735, which is still unrepealed upon the statute books. When you have become a witch you can put the evil eye on your neighbours, make their cattle die, their crops rot.

You do not believe in such nonsense, and neither do I, yet in the picturesque Tudor village of Lower Quinton, its thatched roofs golden among the Cotswold hills, they speak of witches with a wry grin ...

It was Superintendent Alec Spooner of the Warwickshire Constabulary who filled Fabian and Webb in on the myths and customs of the county. According to Fabian, Spooner – quite early in the investigation – gave the London detectives two books to read: Bloom's *Folk Lore, Old Customs and Superstitions in Shakespeare Land*; and Clive Holland's *Warwickshire: The Land of Shakespeare*. Fabian opened the Holland book to a page Spooner had specifically marked:

In the village some interesting and ancient customs still survive, amongst which are the Christmas singers and the crowning of the May Queen. And even as late as 1875 the effect of ancient superstitions concerning witches and the 'Evil Eye' was seen in the crime of a man named John Haywood, who stabbed to death with a pitchfork an old woman eighty years of age, exclaiming whilst he did so that he would kill all the witches in Long Compton, and that there were sixteen of them.

At his trial for murder, during the course of his defence, he said, 'If you had known the number of people who lie in our churchyard, who, if it had not been for them (the witches) would have been alive now, you would be surprised. Her (the deceased) was a proper witch.'

It came out in evidence that this man for years had honestly believed that when cattle or other animals died, or any evil fortune befell his fellow-villagers, such things were the direct result of the 'Evil Eye' of some unfortunate old women he asserted were 'proper old witches'.

His mode of killing the unfortunate old woman he attacked was evidently a survival of the ancient Anglo-Saxon custom of dealing with such persons by means of 'stacung,' or sticking spikes into them; whilst at the same time wishing that the portion of the body so wounded might mortify or wither away.

In the same year as Haywood's crime, a woman who died at Tysoe bore the reputation of being a witch, and was so feared that one day some people came from the neighbouring village of Brailes

with the express intention of nullifying the effects of the 'Evil Eye' she was supposed to have cast upon them by scoring her hand with a corking pin. Shakespeare himself, in the first part of King Henry VI, makes allusion to this practice in the speech of Talbot to Joan of Arc, when the former says:—
Blood will I draw on thee, thou art a witch,
And straightaway give thy soul to him thy servest.

Haywood's victim was Ann Tennant, a life-long resident of Long Compton, who lived in a cottage on Hell Lane with her husband of fifty-six years. For reasons not fully explained, Haywood believed the peasant woman possessed evil, supernatural powers. Tennant crossed paths with Haywood, a farm worker and long-time neighbour, on the evening of 15 September 1875 while walking to the bakery to buy a loaf of bread. The young man was returning from a day in the fields with other labourers and had been drinking cider. Brainwashed by supernaturalism, and drunk, Haywood stabbed Tennant with his pitchfork and beat her about the head. Tennant fell screaming to the ground. A farmer named Taylor, who lived nearby, heard the commotion and ran to the stricken woman's aid. Also drawn by the noise was one of Tennant's seven children, Elizabeth. Taylor restrained Haywood while Elizabeth and others carried the bleeding woman to Elizabeth's cottage. The local police constable turned up shortly thereafter and took Haywood into custody. At eleven o'clock, a doctor summoned from Chipping Norton arrived at Elizabeth's home and found Ann Tennant in a terrible state. The pitchfork had pierced her left temple, the area behind her ear, and numerous spots on both legs. Tennant died while the doctor dressed her wounds.

Haywood, meanwhile, sat in a police cell in nearby Shipston-on-Stour. Questioned by Superintendent James Thompson, Haywood said he had suffered a poor day in the fields and believed Tennant had cursed him. He had every intention, he said, of killing the old woman, and planned to execute the other fifteen witches he claimed lived in the village. When Thompson brought a cup of water to Haywood's cell, the prisoner refused to drink it out of fear 'there were witches in it'. Two days after the murder – 17 September – an inquest into the killing was held at the Red Lion public house in Long Compton. Coroner T.B. Couchman recorded a verdict of 'Willful murder, deliberately stabbed to death by James Haywood [sic] with a pitchfork under the delusion of witchcraft.' Haywood went on trial that December at Warwick Assizes and, due to his perceived mental state, was found guilty of manslaughter. Prior to being shipped off to serve his prison sentence, Haywood told the governor of the gaol in which he was initially incarcerated that the Bible gave him the authority to commit his crime. In all other matters, he was a soft-spoken man – but on the subject of witchcraft, he became loud and visibly excited. He claimed justification for his deeds could be found in Leviticus 20:27:

> A man also or woman that is a medium, or that is a wizard, shall surely be put to death: they shall stone them with stones: their blood shall be upon them.

The details of Tennant's murder – much like those of Walton's – have not escaped embellishment over the years. Subsequent accounts have claimed Tennant was not merely stabbed with a pitchfork but pinned to the ground with the implement. It has also been claimed her assailant used a billhook to slash the sign of the cross into Tennant's prostrate body. A review of records pertaining to the incident prove both assertions to be untrue. This, however, has not stopped numerous authors, among them famed crime writer Colin Wilson, reporting incorrect facts. It could be argued the story of Tennant's slaying has evolved through the years in an attempt to somehow forge a tenuous connection with Walton's death. Conspiracy theorists – and those who believe witchcraft played a role in the 1945 crime – believe both slayings share some mystical bond. This may simply be an attempt to bolster the argument that black magic was indeed a motive in the Lower Quinton case. As it so happens, the Tennant killing is actually mentioned in the Walton case files, but not in the way Fabian presents it in his memoirs. In fact, the murder of Ann Tennant did not come to the attention of Scotland Yard until five years after the Walton murder. If Fabian knew of it beforehand, he kept it out of his official reports.

Perhaps it is no surprise strange stories and theories have attached themselves to Walton's murder, for the land around Lower Quinton – indeed the Cotswolds and Warwickshire – lends itself well to legend, with its rolling hills, narrow lanes, and villages of thatched-roof cottages. By the time he wrote his final book, *The Anatomy of Crime*, Fabian was declaring plain outright the Walton murder had ties to witchcraft:

> A terrible aspect of the entire affair is that the murderer, whoever he or she may be, might still be at liberty and could kill someone else who strays into, or falls foul of, the coven's evil net. I advise anybody who is tempted at any time, and on any pretext, to venture into Black Magic, witchcraft, Satanism – call it what you will – to remember Charles Walton and to think of his death, which was so clearly the ghastly climax of a pagan rite. There is no stronger argument for keeping as far away as possible from the villains with their swords, incense and mumbo-jumbo. It is prudence on which your future peace of mind and even your life could depend.

In the late 1960s, journalist and popular historian Donald McCormick visited Lower Quinton to research the first book on the Walton killing, *Murder by Witchcraft*. McCormick, having already written extensively on crime and espionage, was something of a controversial figure, as his use of anonymous sources made verifying his work difficult. One person he supposedly interviewed for the book was a high priestess in a Warwickshire coven, who claimed that while Walton was not involved in witchcraft, he did possess the ability to communicate with animals:

> There is no evidence whatsoever of sacrificial killings in modern witchcraft ... But fear of witchcraft is hard to remove, harder in some country areas, especially in Warwickshire ... As soon as witchcraft is mentioned as a possible motive in the Lower Quinton murder case, people immediately assume it was ordained by some coven. It was even suggested that Charles Walton was the member of a coven and that he was sentenced to death for revealing its secrets. That is nonsense, too. I assure you the modern practitioners of witchcraft, inside or outside of covens, are not to be found among hedgers and farm labourers. They come mainly from the professional classes and this would have been just as true during the war as today. All I know of witchcraft in this area during the war, when it was very

spasmodically practiced, was that it was partly a form of escape from the rigours of war and, more often, used as invocation for victory. We used the unity of the witches to express through our religion – and it is a religion – our will to defeat the Germans. Some covens used the same technique when the flying bombs came over in the last year of the war. It is of course wicked to accuse this poor old man of being mixed up in some kind of black magic, or to suggest he was malevolently disposed to his neighbours. He was not a member of the cult, though he may have certainly known something about it. What Old Charlie possessed was a strange kind of psychic power which you get in some countrymen. Sometimes it shows in their instinct for amazingly accurate weather forecasting, or for dowsing and divining with hazel twigs. More often – and this was true of Charles – it is revealed in an uncanny understanding of animals and birds and being able to communicate with them.

Walton's slaying was not the first to lend itself to rumours about witchcraft. Another local murder that occurred two years prior – and a mere 40 miles away – was also believed by many to be the result of some grotesque black magic ritual. As with the Lower Quinton crime, it also remains unsolved.

Late on the afternoon of Sunday, 18 April 1943, four boys – Robert Hart, Thomas Willetts, Bob Farmer, and Fred Payne – were hunting for bird nests in Hagley Wood on the stately grounds of Hagley Hall in Worcestershire. The sun was beginning to set, casting long shadows amongst the bare trees near Wychbury Hill. The boys, however, being of adventurous spirit, were not done with their day's outing just yet. As they picked their way over fallen leaves, they spotted a gnarled elm tree in a small clearing. Surely, the boys thought, they might find a nest – perhaps more than one – amongst the tangle of branches. Bob Farmer approached the tree and, having found a satisfactory handhold, clambered up its trunk.

He was roughly 4 feet off the ground when he spotted a large hole in the weathered bark and discovered, while staring into the cavity, the trunk was hollow. Something stared back at him from the tree's cramped confines. Startled, but curious, he leaned in closer and realised he was looking at a skull. Farmer reached into the trunk and attempted to retrieve the grim object. As he tried to pull it out, he noticed patches of human hair still adorned the top of the skull. A ribbon of rotting flesh still clung to the forehead. The eye sockets were hollow, the teeth crooked. Farmer recoiled in horror and disgust, and quickly lowered himself to the ground. The boys were technically poaching and in the woods illegally. Although shocked by their discovery, they decided to keep it amongst themselves. If they went to the police, they might get in trouble for their activities. The boys returned that evening to their respective homes in nearby Stourbridge, all of them having promised not to utter a word about their find to anyone. The youngest of the boys, Thomas Willetts, struggled to keep the secret. Surely, they'd get in greater trouble if it was discovered they knew something about the horror in the woods and hadn't said anything. That night, Thomas told his parents what he and his friends had found. Mr Willetts immediately called the police.

The next morning, the boys met with four officers from the Worcestershire County Police Force and led them into the woods, retracing their steps to the tree, which was not far from the Hagley Road. Sergeant Richard Skerratt climbed the trunk and peered into the cavity. Sure enough, a human skull gazed back at him. He left the other officers to guard the tree and phoned his divisional headquarters, who in turn notified the county's CID. Soon, more officers arrived on the scene, along with Professor James M. Webster – the same pathologist who would perform Charles Walton's autopsy. A police constable produced an axe and chopped away at the cavity, widening it to assist in the removal of the bones. It was immediately obvious that someone had gone to a lot of trouble to conceal the body in the tree. The cavity, at its widest, was only 24 inches. Carefully, Webster removed the remains. In addition to the skull, he pulled from the trunk the victim's spinal column and a shoulder blade. Further down, he found the ribs with a few threadbare scraps of rotted clothing stuck to them. A single crepe-soled shoe was found lying at the bottom of the trunk.

Searching the thick undergrowth around the tree, officers soon discovered a shinbone and, scattered about the area, more scraps of clothing. Buried near the tree, investigators uncovered the finger bones from one of the victim's hands. The recovered remains and the few personal items found – the shoe and a cheap wedding ring, stamped with the words 'rolled gold' – were taken to Webster's laboratory at Birmingham University, where he set about divining what he could from the dead. In a matter of days, he was able to tell the police their victim had been a five-foot-tall woman, about 35 years old. Judging from what remained on her skull, she would have had 'mousy brown hair'. The teeth in her lower jaw were crooked. She had been dead for roughly eighteen months. Perhaps most disturbing was the fact she had given birth at least once. Judging from the wear on the wedding ring, Webster estimated the woman had worn it for at least four years. Using the scraps of clothing found at the scene, he was able to determine what the woman was wearing at the time of her death: 'a knitted woolen cardigan with blue and yellow stripes; a mustard-coloured skirt with a side-fastening zip; a light blue belt; rayon underclothes and black crepe-soled shoes.'

Determining the woman's cause of death proved to be a greater challenge, as the victim's remains showed no obvious signs of physical violence. One vital piece of evidence, however, suggested how the woman may have met her end. Deep in the cavity of the jaw, Webster retrieved a piece of cloth ripped from the woman's cardigan, prompting the pathologist to speculate the woman had died from asphyxiation. To help police identify the woman, Webster constructed a life-sized dummy of the victim, complete with identical clothing and the cheap wedding ring. It became obvious to Webster during his forensic study of the remains that whoever stuck the body in the tree had done so before rigor mortis set in. Considering the width of the cavity in the trunk, it would have been impossible to do otherwise. The opening was too small for anyone but a child to have climbed in there voluntarily. No, someone had forcefully shoved the body, feet first, into the tree – a most difficult task. On 28 April, the coroner of Worcestershire County held an inquest in Stourbridge and returned a verdict of 'murder by some person or persons unknown'.

Initially, police were confident they could easily establish the woman's identity, thanks to Webster's brilliant work. Nevertheless, they realised the case posed one considerable challenge: Roughly a year and a half had passed since the killing. In peacetime, that would be bad enough – wartime Britain, with its heavy civilian casualties, presented an extra level of complexity.

Pictures of Webster's recreation were published in newspapers. While hopefully waiting for a member of the public to step forward with information, detectives began revisiting unsolved 'missing persons' cases. They also checked the Central Air Raid Casualty Bureau to see if anyone matching the victim's description had been reported missing following any air raids. Their search of past police reports did turn up one incident of interest. One evening in July 1941, a local businessman was walking back to his home on Hagley Green. The peaceful nature of his stroll was disrupted by a woman's blood-curdling scream from somewhere deep in the nearby woods. He stopped and listened. The silence immediately following the scream was deafening; the only sound now being the slight rustling of branches in the mild summer breeze. There could be no doubt the scream was human. He walked on, pondering what he should do, when he encountered a schoolteacher walking in the opposite direction. Yes, the schoolteacher had also heard the scream. The two men tracked down a police constable and searched the woods. They found nothing. The timing of the incident struck detectives investigating the murder, for it coincided with Webster's estimation that the woman had been dead for roughly eighteen months. Follow-up queries, however, went nowhere.

Descriptions of the woman's clothing were also sent to manufacturers throughout the country. If police could track down who made the cardigan and other items the woman was wearing, they could then visit the places such items were sold and maybe find a salesperson who remembered the victim. Due to their unique style, the crepe-soled shoes proved easier to trace than the other items of clothing. Detectives tracked all but four pairs of the same type of shoe, which were sold from a market stall in Dudley. Unfortunately, none of their endeavours led to the victim. The publicly released images of Webster's reconstruction were also failing to generate any helpful information. Even dental records – generally a dependable means of identifying a victim – were proving useless. Police hoped the irregular teeth in the woman's lower jaw would provide a lead – but they met with no such luck. 'It seemed,' noted one detective, 'as if the woman had come from another planet.'

While continuing to review police records for anything that might help with the mystery at hand, investigators discovered that a group of gypsies had illegally set up a camp in the woods roughly eighteen months prior. Officers had had to respond one evening to a domestic dispute at the gypsy camp. Was it possible the woman in the tree had been a member of this clan? It would certainly explain why no one seemed to know who she was. Police explored this angle – but, as was starting to become a common theme – could find nothing that lent credence to the theory. Puzzled and increasingly frustrated, detectives momentarily brushed aside what they didn't know and focussed on what they did. The scant evidence they had seemed to suggest a killer with knowledge of the area:

> The disposal of the body took place shortly after death. In addition, the aperture of the wych elm was well disguised and the tree itself was situated in a spot popular with courting couples, ramblers, and picnickers. Even though it was comparatively accessible – less than half a mile from the main road between Birmingham and Kidderminster – it seemed inconceivable that a stranger would seek out such an elaborate hiding place.

None of this, however, explained why the killer hid the body in the fashion he did. Shoving a corpse through an opening nearly 4 feet off the ground would have required considerable physical strength. Was it possible police were looking for more than one individual? Surely, it would have been easier to bury the body in the woods. As 1943 gave way to 1944, police continued to wrestle with the case's numerous unknowns. Strange graffiti, scrawled in chalk, began appearing overnight on walls throughout the West Midlands. 'Who put Luebella down the wych-elm?' read the first message, which appeared in the nearby town of Old Hill. Shortly thereafter, another message – written by the same hand – appeared in Birmingham: 'Hagley Wood Bella.' The message's author eventually settled on 'Who Put Bella Down the Wych Elm?' It was both creepy and somewhat taunting, asking as it did a question the police were no closer to answering than they were the day the body was discovered. Detectives, aware they were most likely dealing with a prankster, nevertheless mined the chalk scribbling for possible clues, specifically in the name. Was 'Luebella' and its shorter derivative, 'Bella,' chosen at random – or did the mystery scribe know something? Was he sending police a hint?

Both names were 'diminutives of Elizabeth' and supposedly common in witchcraft. It was not long before members of the public started to float their own theories regarding 'The Tree Murder Riddle,' as the press had dubbed the crime. Newspapers received letters from readers, suggesting 'Bella' – as the victim was now commonly referred to – had died as part of a black magic ritual. It was a theory born more of local legend than any basis in fact. Hagley Wood, with its long shadows and brooding landscape, had long been rumoured to be haunted. Supposedly, covens gathered deep in the woods for moon-lit rituals and other dark activities. Readers, who claimed to know about such things, said, 'there was a tradition that the spirit of a witch could be successfully imprisoned in a hollow tree'. Indeed, trees play an important role in certain rituals. According to one text:

> Trees are magickal beings, rooted in the earth and extending upward into the sky. The trunk of the tree is a bridge between the worlds. This is why the stump was often used as an altar. It is also why slain gods were hung/sacrificed upon a tree (Lupus, Odin, Quetzalocatl, Jesus, etc.). Here they become the bridge themselves between humankind and the gods. To perform a ritual in front of a tree is to connect with the Underworld (the roots) and with the heavens (through the branches). The old legends say the tree must not be gnarled. This is because evil spirits used to be magickally bound or imprisoned in trees, and the tree became disfigured by the indwelling spirit. Therefore, it was a bad omen to perform a ritual by a gnarled tree.

Some letters to area newspapers pointed out that it was not uncommon in ancient times for certain sects to offer blood sacrifices to damaged trees. The main trunk of the tree in which 'Bella' had been found had been broken off at about 5 ½ feet. Police did not entirely dismiss theories put forward by the public, desperate as they were for leads. They were stymied, however, by a total lack of hard evidence suggesting covens had ever met in Hagley Wood. Even if they had, police could find nothing to prove contemporary witches practiced sacrificial rites. The case hit a seemingly impenetrable dead-end. Like the Walton case, tales of witchcraft and black magic firmly attached themselves to the tragedy.

The Hagley Wood and Lower Quinton crimes would share several occult-related connections. One woman, in particular, would take a keen interest in both tragedies and advance the rumours of witch-craft and evil rituals in both cases to the national press. Margaret Alice Murray was an anthropologist who gained prominence early in her career for her study of Egyptology. As a student of linguistics and anthropology at the University College of London, Murray received no formal study in the history of Egypt. She instead learned and developed her passion for the subject under the tutelage of Sir Flinders Petrie – a pioneer in the preservation of ancient arti-facts – and plied her trade in several archaeological digs in Egypt and Palestine during the 1890s. She eventually earned her doctorate in the field and remained at University College of London for the remainder of her career.

It was in the study of witchcraft, however, that Murray would make a name – albeit a controversial one – for herself. The outbreak of the First World War made it all but impossible for Murray, by now 'a middle-aged and highly-respected Egyptologist with several important academic publications to her name,' to continue work in her chosen field. Restrictions on international travel meant the Land of the Pharaohs was off-limits until the end of hostilities. A woman of great curious intellect, she decided to focus on another subject that had long held her interest: witchcraft. The result, in 1921, was her first book, *The Witch-Cult in Western Europe*, in which she pre-sented her theory asserting 'witches were members of a huge secret society preserving a pre-historic fertility cult through the centuries'. The timing of her book's release proved fortuitous, for Aleister Crowley – The Beast – was becoming a regular feature in British newspapers and generating interest in black magic and the occult. Subsequently, Murray's book sold well and helped establish her as a supposed expert on pagan rituals. In 1929, she cemented her reputa-tion with a commissioned entry on 'Witchcraft' for the *Encyclopedia Britannica*. In the eyes of her subsequent critics, Murray penned the entry in a manner suggesting her own views on black magic, rituals, and the like, was indisputable.

It was Murray who put forward the notion that a coven consists of thirteen individuals – specifically, twelve witches and the devil as its leader. Such a concept was quickly picked up by popular authors of the time, among them Aldous Huxley and Robert Graves, and for-ever worked its way into the public's conscience. In the Hagley Wood murder – and, as will be seen, the Lower Quinton case – Murray found a subject worthy of her attention. The fact the body was discovered in a tree and the victim's severed hand was found buried nearby convinced Murray the murder was a witchcraft killing. In European folklore, the severed hand of an executed person (generally someone who died on the gallows) was believed to possess magical powers. Known as a 'hand of glory,' the grotesque relic could reputedly do everything from opening locked doors to paralysing one's enemies. It could also be used in the casting of a more sinister spell. If the fingertips were set alight, or a candle was placed in the shrivelled palm, the hand would imbue the flame with the power to cast all who saw it into 'a death-like sleep'. The term 'hand of glory' is derived from the French *main de gloire* 'and was related to the mandragora plant, which was believed to have similar narcotic properties'. Murray believed Bella was the victim of a black magic execution, perhaps for crimes committed against a coven. The severed hand, she claimed, certainly supported such a hypothesis. She summed up her theory to a local reporter.

'The very act of placing a body in the hollow of a tree,' she stated, 'is associated with witchcraft. The cult of tree-worship is an ancient one and it is linked with sacrifices. The skeleton alone was left, so one cannot be sure whether the body was marked in any way. The Wych Elm is significant in terms of witchcraft lore. Whoever committed the murder must have known about the hollow in the tree. The other curious fact about this case is that there were many other hollows where the body could have been more easily hidden. As for the chalk writing on walls in Midland towns, these may have been simply the work of a hoaxer or hoaxers. But Lubella, one of the names used, is a witch's name and for that matter so is Bella. Coincidence, perhaps, but strange all the same.'

As with the Lower Quinton murder, the witchcraft angle has overrun the Hagley Wood case and obscured the tragedy of the crime. Most accounts seem to focus more on the elements that suggest a supposed black magic connection than the actual victim. After all, it's easier to draw far-fetched conclusions from the tantalising clues present at the scene than it is to speculate on an individual of whom we know next to nothing. Cut through the mystical hocus-pocus, and the most likely explanation is that 'Bella' died at the hands of a sadistic killer who knew nothing of witchcraft or black magic. But why did he place her in the tree? Perhaps simply because it was an unusual hiding place not likely to be considered in the search for a missing person. And what of the severed hand? Well, that may be nothing more than proof of the killer's brutality. If Bella was the victim of some ritual sacrifice performed by a coven of witches, it's amazing to think no one – in all the time that has passed – broke ranks to reveal what happened in the woods.

The witchcraft theories floated by the public were simply wild speculation. Murray's involvement in the case and her own take on the murder, however, lent credence to the black magic motive. Bella, she proclaimed, 'was another victim of the devil-worshippers'. A decade after the gruesome events in Hagley Wood, Wilfred-Byford Jones – a columnist with the *Wolverhampton Express & Star* – ran a series of articles on the killing under the pseudonym 'Quaestor' (seeker). He tracked down two of the boys – now young men – who had stumbled across the body. Robert Hart and Thomas Willets had no real interest in reliving the experience and refused to revisit the spot in the woods where it all started. He interviewed people in Hagley, who by now considered the stories of witchcraft and rituals to be made-up nonsense. 'I think she was a gypsy,' the vicar's warden told Jones, 'and that she was tried and condemned by her tribe of Romanies.' Jones offered £100 to anyone who could come forward with information that would solve the case. Letters poured in from all over the country – but one, in particular, caught his attention.

The woman signed her name 'Anna' and wrote that Bella, a native of Holland, had been murdered for knowing too much about a German spy ring operating in the Midlands. According to Anna, the spies were gathering intelligence on area munitions factories and passing it onto the Luftwaffe. Anna said the information was being gathered by a British officer and passed along to a Dutchman, who then forwarded it to a one-time trapeze-artist-turned-German spy. Bella, the story went, had come to Britain in 1941 and somehow got mixed up in the intrigue. The Dutchman and trapeze artist, afraid Bella knew too much, lured her into a car one evening, drove to the town of Halesowen and killed her. The body was subsequently placed in the tree in Hagley Wood. The British officer died in an insane asylum in 1942; the fate of the Dutchman and trapeze artist were a mystery. It was certainly not beyond the realm of possibility that spies in the area were pinpointing the locations of munitions factories throughout the Midlands for the Luftwaffe. Indeed, a rumour during the war suggested two Germans had parachuted into the region in 1941 and disappeared under deep cover.

Intrigued by Anna's story, Byford-Jones notified the police, who paid Anna a visit. They were taken by her suggestion that Bella was a foreign national, for this would explain their inability to trace her clothing or identify her through dental records. In a follow-up article, Byford-Jones wrote 'both MI5 and the police investigated her claims'. Some of her story was even 'verified' – but no one was arrested in connection with the crime. The investigation soon dwindled, and the story of Bella in the Wych Elm forever joined the dark and frustrating annals of unsolved crime.

10

No End in Sight

By the end of March, Fabian and Webb had worked every possible angle to their investigation. All the inhabitants of Lower and Upper Quinton had been questioned, as had the Italian POWs in the camp at Long Marston. Police had tracked down every homeless individual in the area and confirmed the whereabouts of all 'mental defectives' in the area. Detectives had travelled to Salisbury, Somerset, and all points beyond and in between to question people they were told had passed through the district on the day Walton died. As thorough as they were, investigators hit dead ends down every avenue they explored.

For Fabian, the Lower Quinton murder was a rare defeat, though he remained confident someone would soon step forward with whatever vital information was needed to solve the crime. The lack of apparent motive continued to frustrate him. Although he still believed money lay at the heart of the crime, he had been unable to produce evidence that confirmed his theory. Subsequent accounts of the crime have not only claimed the motive was financial but have detailed one specific theory as fact. According to these accounts, Potter – short of cash – approached Walton and asked him for a loan. The old man obligingly loaned Potter an undisclosed amount of money. The farmer, thankful, promised to repay Walton by a certain date. When he failed to do so, Walton confronted him. An apologetic Potter promised to have the money soon. When it became apparent Potter had no intention of repaying the loan, Walton got angry. Worried the old man might destroy his reputation, Potter killed Walton to keep him silent and avoid repayment.

'Edith,' claims one account, 'confirmed her uncle had loaned Walton a large sum of money.' If she did tell investigators about the loan, it certainly did not make its way into the official case file. In fact, in a statement she made to Fabian nine days after the murder, she states the exact opposite. 'My uncle always went up to fetch his money from Mr Potter on a Saturday,' she said. 'I never had any idea how much money he drew from Mr Potter, and I never heard him speak of being short or having any difficulty with Mr Potter over his wages. I never heard my uncle say that he had lent any money to anyone, and I have never seen him with any IOUs.' Fabian spent a lot of time checking into Walton's finances and never turned up evidence of any such loan. In fact, according to Scotland Yard documents, Edith – who believed her uncle had several hundred pounds in his bank account – was surprised to find out he actually had very little money. The puzzle surrounding Walton's money – specifically, what happened to it – has never been solved, adding yet another layer of intrigue to the story. Fabian's case report, dated 5 April 1945, concludes:

> The very thorough enquiries made in this case have, so far, uncovered no evidence on which action can be taken. There is suspicion against the farmer Potter, chiefly because of discrepancies in his statements affecting what he says he saw of the murdered man at a time which must have been shortly before the murder.
>
> There are, apparently, no finger impressions on the weapons used. The most positive factor, at present, seems to be the missing watch. It may be that the victim's trousers were undone by the murderer, searching for a money belt. If robbery be the motive, the offender is likely to be a person with local knowledge, although this may not be so.

Fabian returned to London but did not stay there long. He was back in Lower Quinton within a couple of weeks to conduct one last round of questioning, determined to break the case. Upon his return to the Cotswolds, Fabian learned from Warwickshire Constable John West that Potter had returned to the scene of the crime the morning after the killing. Why this information was not relayed to Fabian earlier in the investigation is not known, but the detective immediately acted on it. He drove to The Firs on 18 April to conduct what would be his last interview with Potter.

Not in the mood for customary pleasantries, Fabian asked the farmer outright when did he first visit the field after the killing. Potter responded as though he had just been reminded of some long-forgotten memory.

'I now remember that it was at about half-past eight on the morning of 15th February,' Potter said. 'I went there to have a look at the cattle and sheep.'

'And what happened?' asked Fabian.

Potter said:

When I got there, I saw a policeman in uniform standing by the spot where Charles Walton had been found. He was a stranger to me. I don't think the policeman asked me who I was, and I don't think I told him. I spoke to him about the weather. I think he was the policeman who I told about touching the stale of the trouncing hook. I remember seeing a broken light bulb on the ground, and the policeman told me they had been taking photographs. I gave the policeman a cigarette and after being there about a quarter of an hour, I left and returned home.

The statement seemed to correspond with West's version of events and left Fabian with little to work with. In fact, the whole thing seemed to corroborate some of Potter's earlier statements in which he said he told police shortly after the killing that he touched the trouncing hook. But there was still something odd about the whole thing. 'The most unusual feature of this particular incident,' wrote Fabian in a follow-up report, 'is the fact that Potter, although seen and interrogated by police on several occasions, had never mentioned going to the scene of the crime on the morning after the murder.' Fabian added:

Throughout this enquiry, Potter has repeatedly failed to disclose to police his movements round about the 14th February 1945, until a direct question has been put to him and, in omitting to mention his visit to the scene on the early morning of the 15th February 1945, he has given yet another example of his reluctance to speak of his own actions no matter how innocent they may appear. All this is indicative of a very peculiar mentality.

Implicit in this summary is a question: Why did Fabian never confront Potter and demand an explanation as to the discrepancies in the farmer's various statements? Potter's inability to tell the same story twice remains one of the truly frustrating aspects of the case. Fabian repeatedly mentions Potter's changing story in his official case report but did not take a very aggressive approach when questioning his most likely suspect. One can't help but wonder if Fabian had applied more pressure, would Potter have cracked and revealed whatever it was he wished to hide from the authorities?

Before returning to London, Fabian decided to re-interview a number of villagers in the event they had remembered anything significant about the day Walton died. While no one had anything of substance to add to their original statements, Fabian did consider two recent developments rather interesting. Since Fabian's last visit to the village, two of Potter's farm hands had left his employ – one being Harold Batchelor, the man with whom Potter had crushed mangolds the morning of the murder. Batchelor told Fabian that due to Potter's refusal to give him a raise, he had found a better job elsewhere. The man now seemed uncomfortable discussing his former boss, whereas previously he had no problem supporting Potter's alibi. He averted Fabian's gaze and spoke quietly. 'Whilst I am satisfied that Batchelor's chief reason for leaving Mr Potter is as he states,' Fabian wrote in his case notes, 'I also think it probable that he had been prompted to leave by suspicions he may have formed regarding his former employer's connection with the death of Charles Walton.'

Likewise, Kenneth Eric John Workman, a labourer who had previously told Fabian he had no issues with Potter as an employer or a person, had also changed jobs. 'By his demeanour,' Fabian wrote, 'I am satisfied that he, too, suspects Potter of having some connection with the murder.'

Fabian now returned to London with no more hands to play. In his final case report, Fabian concluded:

For the time being it does not appear that any more can be done in the way of direct enquiries. Wherever possible all persons who could have been in any way implicated in the murder have been interviewed and their movements checked with the result that the only person upon whom the slightest degree of suspicion rests is Potter.

It is not unlikely that the mysteries of the murdered man's money and his death are in some way related but if this is so the most exhaustive enquiries have failed to show us where the connection is.

The local police officers are keeping in close touch with the inhabitants of the district in the hope of bringing to light any such matter as would open up a fresh line of enquiry. If, as I believe, this murder was committed by a local person, I do not think it possible for the matter to end without there being some repercussions which will give rise to an opportunity for us to take such action as may solve the mystery and bring the murderer to justice.

Commander E.R.B. Kemble, chief constable of Warwickshire, thankful for Scotland Yard's intervention, was just as surprised as Fabian by the lack of resolution. In a letter dated 10 April to R.M. Howe, assistant commissioner of Scotland Yard's CID, Kemble wrote, 'If anyone had told me two months ago that murder was going to be committed, and that we should still have no real clue, I should have thought it highly improbable.' The case, however, remained open in the files of Scotland Yard and the Warwickshire Constabulary. Fabian, for his part, was convinced of Potter's guilt. He could think of no other alternative. Indeed, Potter had plenty of opportunity that morning to commit the crime – and his reluctance to come clean about his activities that day, in Fabian's opinion, spoke volumes. But even if taken as circumstantial evidence, it was all too weak to support an arrest. And, as always, there was that nagging lack of clear motive.

Was Potter the killer? He is, judging by official case documentation, the likeliest suspect. Casting aside his apparent inability to honestly disclose what he did the morning of the murder, his statements provide other clues ripe for speculation. In his first statement to Fabian and Webb on 17 February, the farmer told the detectives he saw Walton in the field that morning, working in his shirtsleeves. It's established fact, however, that the victim wore a sleeveless shirt that day. When called on this discrepancy, Potter backtracked and said it couldn't have been Walton that he saw. If operating under the assumption that Potter was the killer, this can be seen as an attempt to mislead police. Potter was trying to bring a third person into play – the supposed murderer. The killer – in this scenario, Potter – had gone through Walton's clothing and would have most likely seen that the old man was wearing a sleeveless shirt beneath his jacket. In telling Fabian and Webb what he saw, he may have wanted the detectives to think that he had actually seen the killer committing the violent deed – and not Walton trimming the hedges. The flipside, of course, is that Potter did actually see Walton at work and mistook the arms of the old man's jacket for shirtsleeves. 'It seems improbable,' Fabian wrote, 'he [Walton] would have worked in shirtsleeves at 12.20 and then put his jacket on, unless he had decided to go home.'

The timing of Potter's supposed sighting is also confusing, as it kept changing. Initially, he told the police he saw the man he believed to be Walton at 12.10 p.m. As we have seen in subsequent statements, Potter told police he saw Walton from a distance at 12.15 p.m., 12.20 p.m., and – finally – 12.30 p.m. It was this time discrepancy that planted Potter squarely in Fabian's sights and left in question Potter's actual movements that morning. That Walton died on Potter's land is not an indication of the farmer's guilt – but one can be sure Potter knew how to get to and from the murder scene without being spotted. If Potter was the killer, did his wife know? Fabian, in his case notes, suggests Lilian and her husband had gone over the morning's events prior to their questioning by police. Again, Mrs Potter couldn't remember certain aspects about the day of the murder – but was very adamant about the times her husband came and went from the house. If she was in on the murder, would she – a quiet, country housewife – have been able to maintain her composure in front of police? It's unlikely considering the state PC Lomasney reports her being in the days following the crime.

And what of Potter going out of his way to explain his possible fingerprints on the murder weapon? Forensic analysis of the trouncing hook and pitchfork failed to turn up any fingerprints – the case file doesn't clarify whether police found no fingerprints at all, or found smudged and partial prints that were unusable. Does this mean the killer wore gloves? If Potter was the murderer, he would have known the answer to that question and wouldn't have needed to worry. If the tools were Potter's – and it's unclear if they were in fact his – one would expect his fingerprints to be found on them. In fact, the use of Walton's working tools in the commissioning of the crime raises questions as to the killer's initial intent. If Potter did indeed enter the field that morning determined to murder the old man, would it not have made more sense to do so already armed with a weapon – something he could have cleaned or disposed of after the crime without raising suspicion? Let's assume for just a moment the motive was an unpaid loan between Walton and Potter. The use of Walton's tools to commit murder suggests a crime of opportunity, rather than one planned in advance. It's not beyond the realm of possibility Potter entered the field hoping to discuss the loan with Walton. Maybe they exchanged a few words and the conversation got heated. One thing led to another and – in a fit of rage – Potter attacked the old man, beating him with the walking stick before wielding the hedging tools with ghastly effect.

To commit such a crime would suggest Potter was a man poisoned by incredible rage, yet there is nothing in the case files to suggest Potter was capable of such violent extremes. Killing in the heat of the moment is one thing, but the particularly savage nature of the Walton slaying points to someone who has what appears to be an uncontrollable bloodlust. While a handful of villagers interviewed by Fabian said Potter could be unpleasant at times – more so, according to one, if he had a few drinks in him – no one ever said he was violent. And even if drinking did bring out a mean side in him, he wasn't drunk when he left the College Arms that morning. In the latter stages of the investigation, Fabian questioned members of the Woman's Land Army who worked on Potter's farm. 'They all say that Potter was kind and considerate to them during their employment with him,' Fabian notes in his report. As Fabian eventually concluded:

> Although the suspicions attached to Potter will be well-appreciated, there is no real evidence to connect him with the murder itself, and no reasonable motive can be found for his committing it. The murder was of a particularly violent and brutal character and there is not the slightest evidence that Potter is of a violent disposition. Neither is there any suggestion that he and Walton had ever quarrelled.

Walton's murder was an example of overkill, which generally means the crime was personal with anger or hatred fuelling the violence.

Jack the Ripper was most likely driven by a hatred of women – or, specifically, prostitutes. What was it about Walton that spurred his killer to such grisly extremes? Criminal profiling was still a burgeoning science in the 1940s, having first come into play during the Ripper investigation. A basic tenet of modern-day profiling is assessing the crime scene to classify what type of offender one is dealing with. One such offender is the 'Disorganised Offender'. This person often acts on impulse, striking out without warning and overwhelming the victim with violent force. Because the Disorganised Offender doesn't plan ahead, they don't carry their own weapons, opting instead to use whatever implements are available at the scene of their crime – as Walton's killer did. If their particular crime is homicide, they'll make no effort to hide the body or dispose of the murder weapons. In some cases, this type of offender will indulge in some sort of sexual contact with the victim. It will be remembered that Walton's clothes – including his trousers – were undone, though if someone were searching for the money Walton was rumoured to carry around with him, this would be expected.

The Disorganised Offender is young – usually in their twenties – has a spotty employment record and works at menial jobs. They also have a hard time maintaining intimate relationships and may live alone or with a relative. The *modus operandi* of the Disorganised Offender lend themselves well to the Lower Quinton murder, yet none of the offender's characteristics fit Potter, adding to the frustrating nature of the case. For while it's easy to present circumstantial evidence to support theories that Potter was the killer, it's impossible to pin anything definitive on him. In the end, the argument favouring Potter as the killer relies primarily on his strange behaviour after the killing and the window of opportunity he apparently had to commit the crime that morning.

In his final volume of memoirs, published twenty-five years after the killing, Fabian wrote: 'I have never said this publicly before, but I *think* I know who did it. Who, though, will come forward with the evidence?' Obviously, he could not identify Potter by name due to libel laws. The farmer was still alive. After his retirement, however, Fabian told crime writer Richard Whittington-Egan in private conversation, he believed wholeheartedly Potter was the killer.

❋

The case remained all but inactive for the next three years. In Warwickshire, Superintendent Alec Spooner maintained casual contact with villagers but came no closer to solving the crime. In August 1948, however, he stumbled across one possible lead he hoped might shed light on things. Through a fellow officer with the police in Skegness, Lincolnshire, Spooner learned a stick-up man named Ernest Roy Smith was awaiting trial at the Lincolnshire Assizes 'on a joint charge of burglary, involving property to the value of £777 by "hold-up" methods'. The address Smith had provided police upon his arrest was in Upper Quinton. On 28 August, Spooner sent a letter to the Superintendent of County Police, Lincolnshire, detailing the Walton murder and describing the dead man's missing pocket watch:

> Although there is no evidence whatever to connect Smith with the offence committed in this district, it would appear to be desirable in all the circumstances that his movements during the material times should be carefully checked, and I should be obliged if you would kindly allow an experienced officer to interview Smith with a view to ascertaining his movements at the time of the murder and acquaint me with the results in due course. At the same time, perhaps you will kindly cause the property found in Smith's possession upon arrest for your offence to be checked to see whether he has a watch similar to that described above.

The Lincolnshire authorities kindly obliged Spooner's request – but, in the end, could find nothing to connect Smith with Walton's death. There would be no more significant activity in the case file for another two years.

※

Fabian, meanwhile, garnered more celebratory headlines in 1946 after successfully investigating the murder of Dagmar Peters, whose strangled corpse was found on Halloween alongside the A20 Maidstone to London road. The settling of blood in the body indicated the woman had died in a sitting position and remained that way for some time after death. Through family, Fabian learned that 48-year-old Dagmar often hitched rides on the A20 to visit her sister-in-law in London. She always went out carrying a yellow string bag – but no such bag had been found near the body. Obviously, Fabian theorised, someone had picked her up, killed her, taken the bag, and dumped the body along the road.

Dagmar's sister-in-law had knitted the yellow string bag as a gift. Fabian asked her to make another identical one, which he then had photographed and published in national newspapers. A 15-year-old boy, who saw one of the pictures, contacted Scotland Yard and said he found a bag just like it in Clare Park Lake on 3 November, three days after the killing. Several hairs – one belonging to Dagmar's sis-ter-in-law, and another belonging to Dagmar's puppy – were found when the bag was examined at the police laboratory in Hendon. Surveying the area around Clare Park, Fabian guessed 'the bag had been thrown into a stream which fed through a culvert under a fac-tory and into Clare Park Lake'. Fabian interviewed the factory fore-man and learned a truckload of bricks had recently been delivered. The driver's name, the foreman said, was Harold Hagger. A call to the Yard's Criminal Record Office revealed Hagger was no stranger to the judicial system, having been convicted of sixteen crimes in the past, including an assault on a woman. When confronted by Fabian, Hagger said Dagmar had tried to steal his wallet after he picked her up on the A20. He pulled at her scarf to try and stop her – but pulled too tight. The death, he claimed, was an accident. Fabian did not buy Hagger's story – and neither did the subsequent judge who sent Hagger to the gallows.

Fabian was by now nearing retirement. From his office on the third floor of Scotland Yard's gothic-looking headquarters on Victoria Embankment, he could look out his window at the city he had come to know so well. 'I have no doubts,' he would later write, 'that if I had my life over again, I wouldn't change it for any other.' Violence would beckon him into the streets one last time for one of post-war London's more infamous killings. On the afternoon of 29 April 1946, three masked men, all armed, stormed into Jay's, a jeweller's shop at 73–75 Charlotte Street. One bandit leapt over the counter and, with the barrel of his pistol, savagely beat the company director about the head, knocking him to the floor in a pool of blood. The 70-year-old store manager threw a large, wooden stool at the robbers in an attempt to dissuade them. A muzzle flashed and a gun roared; the slug just missed the manager and buried itself in the wall. Panicked and empty-handed, the culprits fled outside only to find their getaway car blocked in by a lorry. The men, their features still obscured by masks, abandoned their car and ran down the street past startled onlookers. Just at that moment, 30-year-old Alec de Antiquis, a married father of six, manoeuvred his motorcycle around the lorry and saw the gunmen making their escape. He revved the throttle and skidded the bike across the roadway, blocking their escape route. Without hesitation, one of the bandits shot Antiquis in the left temple between the ear and eyebrow. Antiquis fell into the gutter.

Fabian was having lunch that afternoon at the Colonial Club when the call came in. He abandoned his meal and quickly made his way to Charlotte Street, where he found the abandoned getaway car and nearly thirty witnesses ready to provide statements. Antiquis had been taken by ambulance to the hospital, but the wound proved fatal. Despite what appeared to be an abundance of evidence, the crime scene surrendered few clues. An extensive dusting of the getaway car failed to produce any usable prints – and, despite the number of people who witnessed the shooting, no one could agree on what the gunmen looked like. A break came a couple of days later when a taxi driver walked into the police station on Tottenham Court Road and said a young man with a handkerchief tied around his neck had hopped onto the running board of his cab shortly after the murder. The cabbie told the stowaway to get lost and watched as the man darted across the street and disappeared into a building at 191 Tottenham Court Road.

Early the next morning, Fabian – and several other detectives from the Flying Squad – arrived at the address in an undercover police car. The building, it turned out, was an office block. Fabian and his men began a thorough search of the offices. In a vacant room on the top floor, they found a raincoat, cap, a pair of gloves, and a scarf – knotted at both ends – and folded into a triangle to make a mask. Fabian noticed the manufacturing labels had been torn out of the cap and the raincoat. Tearing away the raincoat's inner lining, however, he found sewn into the seam a stock ticket for a clothing company based in Leeds. A call to the factory revealed the coat had been delivered to one of three possible shops in London. The first two shops proved to be a dead end. The third shop was on the Deptford high street. Fabian showed the coat to the store manager, who said he sold it to a customer several months prior. The manager gave Fabian the address for a block of flats in Bermondsey. The trail led Fabian to the home of the Jenkins family, a clan with a criminal past. The eldest son was serving time for robbing a London jewellery store; the other son, Harry, had been convicted on two separate occasions for assaulting police officers, breaking the jaw of one constable. The leader of a local gang and known on the street as 'The King of Borstal', Jenkins had only been released from Borstal prison a mere six days before the Antiquis murder.

Fabian, confident he had his killer, brought Jenkins in to take part in a line-up. Not one of the twenty-seven witnesses from Charlotte Street could pick Jenkins out. Fabian had no choice but to let his prime suspect go, though he harboured no doubt Jenkins was the killer. Fabian assigned detectives to shadow Jenkins and those he associated with. In the meantime, a schoolboy wandering along the muddy banks of the Thames in Wapping found a gun protruding from the muck. Scotland Yard's firearms expert matched the weapon to the bullet taken from Antiquis's body by comparing the grooves on the slug to the rifling in the gun's barrel. Much to Fabian's chagrin, however, there were no prints on the weapon and no way to link it to Jenkins.

The investigation had now been ongoing for several days and was taking a physical toll on Fabian. 'My clothes were rumpled,' he later recalled, 'dishevelled from days of camping out at the police station, my cheeks were raw from shaving with ordinary soap as I had not even taken time to telephone home for my toilet kit, and my eyes were gritty with sleep.' But the thought of the victim's six children – and Antiquis himself, bleeding to death in the gutter – made it easy for Fabian to push through the fatigue. He was now receiving frequent updates from the team of detectives following Jenkins and his associates. Not long after Fabian let him go, Jenkins was spied in a pub drinking at a table with two other young men police subsequently identified as 17-year-old Terence Peter Rolt and 21-year-old Christopher James Geraghty. Detectives stuck to all three men, keeping a watch on their daily routines.

Several days after the first gun was found, another schoolboy found a .45 revolver alongside the Thames in Wapping. Forensic analysis determined the gun had fired the shot that wound up in the wall inside the store. Fabian could not help but notice both guns were found less than a quarter of a mile from the home of Jenkins's mother-and father-in-law. Unfortunately, it was still not enough to make an arrest. Detectives, however, caught a break after they tracked down a one-time associate of Jenkins. A thief named Bill Walsh told investigators he had staked out the jewellery store for Jenkins and Geraghty five days before the robbery but did not take part in the actual crime. Acting immediately on the information, Fabian arrested Geraghty. The date was 17 May. The young man tried to play it cool under questioning, casually smoking his cigarettes and shrugging off the accusations against him. From the police surveillance, Fabian knew Geraghty was good friends with Jenkins and would most likely do his best to protect him. He had no such loyalty, however, when it came to young Rolt. Geraghty gave a statement implicating himself and Rolt in the stick-up job, but never once mentioned Jenkins.

Two days before the attempted robbery, Geraghty said, he and Rolt broke into a gunsmith's after-hours near the Borough Tube Station and robbed the place of several pistols and rounds of ammunition. On the day of the robbery, a Tuesday, Geraghty and Rolt – along with a third accomplice who Geraghty said he couldn't name – met at the Whitechapel Tube Station. They had lunch in a café near the jewellery shop. When they had finished their meal, Rolt and the unnamed accomplice went to steal a car before meeting Geraghty outside the shop. The robbery was a fiasco. As they fled, it was Geraghty who shot Antiquis.

At 2.30 a.m. in the morning of 18 May, Fabian knocked on the door of the Rolt family's flat and took the frightened teen into custody. Rolt pleaded with detectives not to wake up his mother as they led him away. Scared of his impending fate, he had no problem giving up Jenkins and identifying him as the mastermind. It was all Fabian needed to arrest Jenkins the next day. All three were formally indicted on a charge of murder on 19 May. Still a minor, Rolt was spared the gallows and sentenced to a minimum term of five years. Geraghty and Jenkins rendezvoused with the hangman at Pentonville Prison on 19 September. The Antiquis murder was the second time in as many years the Jenkins family name was linked to a high-profile killing. On 8 December 1944, three masked men smashed the window of a jewellery shop in Birchin Lane and grabbed more than £2,000 in merchandise. They ran back to their waiting Vauxhall and sped off down the narrow street. At that moment, Royal Navy Captain Ralph Binney stepped into the car's path and raised his hand in an attempt to stop the vehicle. The black Vauxhall ploughed over Binney and dragged him for more than a mile before his body became disentangled from the car's undercarriage. Binney died from his injuries. One of the men eventually arrested in connection with the robbery and Binney's death was Thomas James Jenkins – Harry Jenkins's brother. Because he was not driving the vehicle, Jenkins was charged with manslaughter and sentenced to eight years in prison.

The Antiquis case was, in the words of one Scotland Yard historian, 'a fitting end to a tremendous career'. Although Fabian still had three years left until his retirement, it proved to be his last major case in the national spotlight.

THE MYSTERY'S ALLURE

For all of Fabian's spectacular successes – and his doubtless skill as
a detective – history has deemed the murder of Charles Walton his
most famous case for its seemingly impenetrable mystery. The mys-
tique only deepens if Potter is innocent, for then we have no suspect
on which to build a theory. Unsolved murders continue to intrigue,
for they dare us to play detective. The Jack the Ripper killings have
held our fascination for more than a century because their gruesome
story lacks a proper ending. The crimes tantalise the imagination and
prod us to wonder who would be capable of such barbarity. New
theories are routinely put forward, yet we know there's no real possibility of truly solving the crime – and therefore the mystery remains.
The same can be said for what has become known as the 'Lower
Quinton Pitchfork Murder'. The public took a keen interest in the
crime, for the nature of the killing struck a chord. Who would do
such a thing to a crippled old man? Some wrote letters to police
putting forward their own theories. One in particular stated, 'It is
almost certain that the murderer is either a landowner, or the owner
of cattle or sheep. Quite possibly he mistook a harmless "white"
witch, which is what the murdered man may well have been, for a
"black" witch.' The letter went on to explain the killer may have
killed Walton because of a curse placed on crops or livestock. Some
accounts point out the fact that one of Potter's heifers drowned in a
brook the day before the murder and that Potter subsequently killed
the old man to avenge the death. This, however, begs the question:

Why would Potter ever have employed a man whom he believed to be a witch?

Indeed, the many distortions and fabrications surrounding the case start with Walton himself. Depending on what account you read, the victim was a quiet old man who kept to himself – or a demented warlock who possessed the ability to communicate with animals. He is painted as a recluse, a witch, or both. Indeed, one case study declares, 'Walton had quite a sinister reputation in the village, where it was common knowledge that he bred huge toads and was once a legendary horse whisperer.' According to this account, 'Walton had been seen on many occasions imitating the songs of the nightingale and chirping to other species of bird. He openly professed to be conversant in the Aeolian language of his feathered friends, for they seemed to obey his requests to refrain from eating the seeds sown in the fields of his little plot.'

The Encyclopedia of Witchcraft, Witches and Wicca also alludes to Walton's supposed ability to control animals. Walton 'was widely known to have clairvoyant powers and claimed he could talk to birds and direct them to go wherever he wanted, simply by pointing. He also claimed to have a lesser control over animals, except dogs, which he feared. He bred large toads of a type called "natterjack", which runs rather than hops.' Famed crime and occult historian Colin Wilson claims Walton's garden was overrun with toads at the time of his death. One account asserts Walton bred 'demonic toads'. It was believed in early times that natterjack toads, known for a distinctive yellow stripe that runs down their back, were a particular favourite of witches. Consequently, such animals were burned 'as creatures of the devil' in sixteenth-century England.

The witchcraft angle slowly gained credence with the passage of time. In 1950, Dr Margaret Murray decided to undertake her own investigation. She travelled from London to Lower Quinton and posed as an artist, moving about the countryside with a sketchbook and pencils. She engaged the villagers of Lower Quinton in casual conversation, working the murder of Charles Walton into her discussions, posing as nothing more than a curious traveller. As with the Hagley Wood murder, she believed dark forces were at play amidst the quaint setting of the Cotswolds. Her views were published in the *Birmingham Post*:

I think there are still remnants of witchcraft in isolated parts of Great Britain and I believe that Charles Walton was one of the people sacrificed. I think this because of the peculiar way in which he had been killed. His throat had been cut and a pitch-fork had been used after he was dead to prevent him from being moved. The sacrifices are carried out by people who still believe in a religion practised in Britain before Christianity whom we call devil-worshippers. They still practise Black Magic. The belief is that if life is taken out of the ground through farming it must be replaced by a blood sacrifice. I am not interested in the murder, only in the witches. I think it was a murder without normal motive – no money was missing and there was no other reason why the old man should have been killed.

Here, we see she alludes to 'life being taken out of the ground'. This harkens back to a theory, put forward by some, that Walton used his supposed menagerie of demonic toads for evil means. The aforementioned Donald McCormick in his book *Murder by Witchcraft* seemed to support this notion. McCormick published an interview with an individual he claimed to be a retired farmer from Long Compton who had employed Walton on several occasions. The farmer did not want his name published, so the book refers to him as 'Mr Blank'. In it, Mr Blank claimed Walton believed in the magical power of toads:

He wouldn't kill them. Now the toads we get in England are not large, not more than three and a half inches as a rule, and the female ones are largest. Now, if you get a natterjack toad, the legs are so short they can't hop, but they can run quite fast. Old Charlie used to catch a toad and tie a toy plough to its legs and have it run along towing the thing across a field.

This is a direct reference to the old witchcraft practice of 'blasting,' a power or ability used by witches 'to interfere with or destroy the fertility of man, beast and crop'. As previously noted, infamous Scottish witch Isobel Gowdie – who went on trial for her practicing of black magic in 1662 – blasted crops by yoking frogs to small ploughs and making them run through local fields, thus sterilising the soil. It's stated in some accounts that the 1944 crop season in Lower Quinton was bad – and 1945 was expected to be no better. Many books have stated villagers blamed Walton for the bad crops, believing he harnessed his toads to toy ploughs and sent them through the fields to wreak havoc with local farmers. This, of course, is absurd. Nowhere in the official case files does it allude to Walton owning toads, let alone harnessing them to miniature ploughs. None of the locals spoke of such odd behaviour. Even Fabian, who played up the witchcraft angle in his memoirs, makes no mention of this. The facts aside, why would Walton – if he were capable of such a thing – destroy the very land he depended on for his livelihood?

Nevertheless, most published accounts of the Walton murder allude to the man's supposed powers of witchcraft; many suggest the villagers were scared of him. The Scotland Yard files do not support these theories. While the statements of residents in Lower Quinton confirm Walton preferred his own company, not once do they allude to evil toads, subservient fowl, or black magic. He is, as we have seen, remembered as a pleasant, quiet man. It's safe to assume that if people feared Walton was a practising warlock, surely one person would have said something. If the person who murdered Walton believed the man to be a practitioner of black magic and intended to kill him that morning, would they have entered the field unarmed? The police reports filed by Fabian during the course of his inquiry not once mention any suspicions that Walton was a practicing witch.

In the wake of Margaret Murray's visit to Lower Quinton and the publication of her comments in the press, a letter from one Mrs Tennant of Allesley, near Coventry, reached the offices of the Chief Constable, Warwick. In the letter, the woman said she was a distant relative of Ann Tennant, the woman murdered by the pitchfork-wielding John Haywood in Long Compton in 1875. She went on to explain that 'Haywood believed [Ann] had an "evil eye",' which she supposedly used to kill one of his pigs simply by looking at it. He became so enraged, he stabbed the old woman with his pitchfork. 'This method of killing,' Mrs Tennant wrote, 'was evidently a survival of an ancient Anglo Saxon custom of dealing with persons by means of sticking spikes into them.' The Warwickshire Constabulary was intrigued by the information and interviewed the woman, who said she had no firsthand knowledge of the Long Compton affair. Her sister-in-law in London, however, remembered the incident. The Warwick police forwarded the information to Scotland Yard, noting:

In the murder at [Lower] Quinton, the dead man was pinned to the ground by a pitchfork, and it is known that a local man, who was a suspect in the case, had a heifer die on the 13th February (the day previous to the murder). Whether these similarities mean anything we do not know.

The sister-in-law, 80-year-old Agnes Pullinger, lived in Hammersmith. Scotland Yard Superintendent G. Mahon questioned her on the morning of 4 April 1950. Here is her statement in its entirety:

When I was five years of age, I was living in the village of Long Compton, Warwickshire, with my parents whose name was Tennant.

In the summer of 1875, I remember my father telling me about a man having murdered my grandmother, who was also named Tennant. I believe the man's name was Haywood. The story I heard was that Haywood killed my grandmother by driving the prongs of a pitchfork into her stomach. She was in the village street during the evening and the man went up to her and killed her without warning – and, as far as I know, for no reason whatever. I remember her as a very charming old lady.

I did not see the body of the murdered lady, but I remember seeing the man Haywood being taken away by policemen in uniform. He was kept in Long Compton lock-up all night and then was taken to Shipston-on-Stour. It was when he was removed from the lock-up that I saw him. Later, I heard that Haywood was found to be insane, and so he was not hanged.

I believe he was a farm labourer. Although I was only 5 years of age when the murder was committed, I remember some of the details I have given quite clearly.

Because the old woman believed her grandmother was killed for no discernible reason, Mahon saw no need to tell her Haywood believed the victim was a witch empowered by an 'evil eye'. The detective, in fact, thought little of the story. Agnes, by her own admission, was only 5 when the murder took place – and childhood memories can easily be distorted as one grows older. In a quiet village such as Long Compton, stories about the murder would have undoubtedly been told for years to come. It would have been all but impossible at the time for the young Agnes not to hear some of what the locals were saying. It's not inconceivable such talk coloured her version of events. And while an interesting story, there was not much Scotland Yard could do with it. This was a crime that occurred seventy years before the Walton slaying. If the Warwickshire Constabulary wanted to investigate the matter further, Mahon suggested additional details might be found in newspapers from the period.

And there, as far as the police were concerned, any tenuous connection between the Tennant and Walton murders came to an end. In the public sphere, however, the crimes have become intrinsically linked. Multiple accounts have since stressed the supposed similarities between the two killings. One article notes:

> [Tennant's] killing could hardly have been more public or more brazen. As she went to the local baker's shop to buy a loaf of bread for her husband's tea, a man stepped forward, thrust his pitchfork through her throat pinning her to the ground and then carved bloody crucifixes on her face and chest with a bill hook.

As we have seen in the Scotland Yard files, Walton's killer did not carve the sign of the cross into the dead man's flesh – nor did Haywood disfigure his victim in such a fashion. The only similarity between the two killings is the use of a pitchfork. Even then, the crimes are not identical. Tennant was attacked on a street in front of witnesses and stabbed multiple times in the legs. She was not pinned to the ground or cut with a slash hook.

Publicly, the Tennant killing became linked to Walton's death in 1954. On 13 February, one day before the ninth anniversary of Walton's murder, the *Daily Mirror* ran a feature story on the Lower Quinton case. 'Ask in these parts whether seventy-four-year-old Charles Walton, murdered in a hedgerow here nine years ago on Sunday, was the victim of witchcraft, and even the detectives no longer smile,' the article began:

> For I can reveal that new clues and strange coincidences in this unsolved crime have recently come to light. And the idea that Walton was a twentieth-century sacrifice to black magic is no longer a joke in this Warwickshire hamlet. At the time it seemed

quite a commonplace murder. Walton, a hedger, was found with his throat slashed, beneath the hedge he had been trimming. 'Just find the motive and you find the killer,' thought the police. But whispers of black magic trickled round the cottages of Lower Quinton almost as soon as Superintendent Alex [sic] Spooner, chief of Warwickshire C.I.D., and Superintendent Bob Fabian of The Yard started their enquiries.

The article detailed the crime and stuck, for the most part, with the facts before veering into speculation. 'Now,' wrote the reporter, 'here are some of the coincidences that have come to light':

The Date. According to the old-time calendar, which is thirteen days behind the present one, the killing took place on February 1 – the eve of a traditional sacrificial day. On that day a human being was killed in the belief that his life blood dripping into the ground would replace the fertility taken from the soil by the previous season's crops.

The Method. The killer first threw the frail old man to the ground and then, before slashing him, pinioned him by the neck with the two prongs of his hayfork. Then the fork haft was forced over and wedged at an angle – almost as though to make certain that his blood would flow to the ground.

The Previous Murder. In 1875 at Long Compton, only a day's tramp across the Cotswold foothills, eighty-year-old Ann Tennant was the victim of one of the last known witch killings. She was killed with a two-pronged hayfork.

The police have found one other link between the killings, but I am pledged not to reveal it.

On that last point, one can only speculate as to the supposed link the police had uncovered, for there is nothing in the Scotland Yard file indicating any connection between the two killings. Some have speculated Ann Tennant and Charles Walton were distant relatives. Surely, if detectives discovered a family connection between the two it would have been thoroughly investigated. While this does not appear to be the case, genealogical research reveals there is an extremely tenuous connection between Tennant and Walton. Their two families are distantly connected by a single marriage, but they are not blood relations. The Cotswolds are a rural area – even more so back in the 1800s. It's not a stretch to say you could easily find a connection between many families from the area if one digs back far enough.

The article also references the date of the murder, claiming Walton died on the eve of what, in times long past, was a day of sacrifice. This was the first time the date of the killing had been given any special significance. The Scotland Yard case files mention no such fact, yet it's one that has gained traction over time. The self-professed witch expert Margaret Murray lent credence to the theory in an interview on 1 June 1956 with a writer for *Reveille*. She said:

The lack of a motive was puzzling. There was also the significance of the day – the 14th of February. In pre-Christian times, February was a sacrificial month, when the soil was spring-cleaned of the dirt of winter. In the old calendar, February 2nd was a sacrificial day, but the old calendar was 12 days behind ours, which means that February 14th corresponds to February 2nd. But I found nothing to support my theory beyond that. The pitchfork was never an instrument of sacrifice in this country, though it may have been in Italy – and there were Italian prisoners of war in the neighbourhood at the time.

Murray's old calendar calculations and those of the newspaper are off by one day – though it hardly matters, for the theory has no basis in reality. It has subsequently been claimed that Valentine's Day, if going by the aforementioned 'old calendar,' is a witches' sabbath. In his book, *The Meaning of Witchcraft*, the late Gerald Brosseau Gardner, an instrumental figure in bringing contemporary Wicca to the public's attention, writes that witches' sabbaths 'relate to the Sun, the Moon, and the Zodiac. Hence, St. Valentine's Day is not a witches' Sabbat, though it was originally a pagan festival.' In other words, the date of the murder is completely irrelevant. Also weakening Murray's theory the murder was motivated by witchcraft is her suggestion Walton died at the hands of an Italian POW. If an Italian did kill the old man, it means the murder had nothing to do with old English black magic rituals.

✳

As with any unsolved murder, the Walton killing was the focus of much conjecture. Amateur sleuths, ghost hunters, psychics, and bored housewives all had theories as to who killed Walton and why. On 27 November 1952, sixteen members of the Birmingham Psychic Society decided the time was right to try and make contact with Walton beyond the grave. Their efforts were encouraged by a local parish councillor, who, highly disturbed by the violent nature of Walton's death and the rumours that swirled about the crime, wanted answers once and for all. Accompanying the party from the psychic society was a reporter from the *Birmingham Post*. It seemed an appropriate day for trying to contact the dead. When the group arrived in Lower Quinton that afternoon, the sky was leaden, and a cold wind blew through the village. The small group made their way into the fields and began climbing up Meon Hill. The parish councillor, Tony Mills, led the way, hoping to conduct the séance at the site of the murder.* Wrote the reporter:

> Shortly after we started, a blizzard began and sleet fell. At length baffled by the darkness of the night, Mr Mills could not find the exact spot where the murder was committed. The other members of the party, knowing they were in a short distance from it, decided to hold their séance at the point they had reached.
>
> The medium, Mrs Hickinbottam of Birmingham, went into a trance and appeared to be speaking of a man named Walton. She pronounced: 'I forgive, I forgive. I deserved what was coming to me, but not in such a brutal way.'
>
> After about ten minutes and some intelligible words, the medium came round supported by her friends to prevent her falling.
>
> Meanwhile, Mr Mills had found the white gate by which the body was found, not fifty yards from the place under a gnarled old willow tree, blown about in the fury of the storm. When Mr Mills told the medium how near she had been to the exact position of the murder she remarked: 'The blow was struck by the tree.'

---

* It's most likely they conducted their séance in the wrong place, judging by the reporter's description.

The party then turned for the two-mile trudge back to their cars in the village.

It's an account that seems more apropos of a bad reality television show. And so, despite the psychic society's best efforts, the mystery surrounding Walton's death lingered. Mr Mills, however, continued his investigation, determined to find out what happened that day near Meon Hill. He would later say he believed his quest for the truth disturbed some supernatural force of evil. After collecting a soil sample from what he believed to be the murder site to have it analysed by a laboratory, Mills claimed a black cloud descended on his home in Moreton Morrell. He sprained his ankle, his daughter came down with pneumonia – not once, but twice – and forty of his sixty-five chickens mysteriously died. Once he got rid of the soil, of which a close analysis turned up nothing out of the ordinary, the misfortune stopped.

In February 1956, four years after the Birmingham Psychic Society's efforts on Meon Hill, several stories about the killing made their way into Midland newspapers. The first ran in the *Daily Herald* on 15 February under the headline, 'Police Chief Goes Back on the Witches' Sabbat.' The police official in question was Detective-Superintendent Alec Spooner of the Warwickshire Constabulary. The fact Walton's killer remained at large rankled the detective, who refused to believe the culprit's identity remained unknown in the village. The mystery became something of a minor obsession for Spooner, who began visiting Lower Quinton every year on the anniversary of Walton's death. On each occasion, he strolled the quiet streets, stopped by the College Arms, and chatted with the locals. 'I let myself be seen,' he later recalled. 'If the murderer is about, he wants the crime forgotten.' Having walked the village, Spooner would make his way through the churchyard and into the fields, to the spot where Walton died. There, he would bow his head in a moment of silence and, when done, take in the scene. The serenity of the place had a dark undercurrent. It seemed odd, standing in that quiet corner of England, contrasting the quiet village nearby with its thatched roofs and smoking chimneys, to the barbarity that took Charles Walton's life. The event did not fit the surroundings.

Whereas the Birmingham Psychic Society sought to find answers to the Walton mystery, one woman claimed to not only know who did it, but confessed to playing a minor role in the tragedy. Shortly after the *Herald* article appeared, the woman – who spoke on the condition of anonymity – contacted several papers in the Midlands and said she knew who killed Walton. On 19 February, the *Reynolds News* ran her story:

A terrified woman, driven nearly grey-haired by some of the most evil men in Britain, offered last night to help solve the murder of Charles Walton, who was impaled with a pitchfork in a lonely Warwickshire field on St. Valentine's Day, 1945. She will give the name of the alleged murderer to Det. Supt. A. W. Spooner, Chief of the Warwickshire C.I.D. ...

This woman, who begged me not to reveal her name, has offered to tell Det. Supt. Spooner everything – provided she is protected from the vengeance of Britain's black magic cults ...

For twelve frightful years she took part with other members of the cult in grotesque rites that stem from Britain's mysterious past. Now she wants the police to stamp out these evil practices. And she wants them to solve the 11-year-old crime she claims was a ritual murder.

Three or four survivors of an ancient cult live in the locality, she said, but the actual murderer was a woman who was brought by car from a different part of the country. The leader of the London cult was present.

'This was revealed to me by the Midlands leader who wants Number One out of the way so that he can gain control. Their numbers are increasing in the Midlands.'

The following day, 20 February, the *News Chronicle* went to press with the woman's account under the headline, 'Murder at Black Mass, says Woman':

A woman has come forward to say that a shepherd, killed eleven years ago, was murdered by a woman during a Black Mass at midnight. She says that she was once a member of a black magic society and that she knows the name of the killer. The body of the shepherd, 74-year-old Charles Walton, was found on St Valentine's Day, 1945, in the middle of a circle of stones in a field at Lower Quinton, Warwickshire. He had been killed by blows from a farm billhook and staked to the ground with a pitchfork. His neck was slashed in the shape of a cross. Villagers said it was a ritual murder. There was a similar murder on St Valentine's Day, 1875, Long Compton, also in Warwickshire. The accuser, an elderly woman from Birmingham, will probably be interviewed by police this week.

It's clear from the reported details, the woman had no inside knowledge of the crime. That she knew a pitchfork and billhook were used in the killing suggested nothing, as such information had been widely reported in the papers. As we know, Walton was killed midday – not at midnight. Nowhere did his flesh bare the bloody sign of the cross, nor was his body found in the centre of a stone circle. There are no stone circles within sight of where Walton died. Lastly, the victim was not a shepherd. Even the brief reference to the Tennant murder is factually inaccurate, as the old woman was murdered on 17 September 1875. There is nothing in the Scotland Yard case file to say the police spoke to the reporter's informant – but why would they? It's clear from the article she knew nothing about the crime. That, however, did nothing to stop her from publicising her story. On 15 March, the *Daily Mirror* ran a story headlined 'Black Magic Murder'. Although she still claimed Walton had died during a black mass ritual, she had clearly brushed up on some of the facts about the case, as several details had now changed:

> Thirteen people took part in the ceremony. One of them knew Walton. The rest came from various parts of the country. Walton was hedging that day in a field well away from houses and the road. The person who knew him approached him with two others. He was struck down. It was exactly midday. Rapidly they mutilated his body, soaked some robes in his blood, drove in the pitchfork, and danced round the body.

She's right that Walton was murdered during the daytime, though he did not die at *exactly midday*. The spot where Walton was attacked is not completely isolated. From the corner of the field where Walton died, one can see the Lower Quinton churchyard and nearby houses. Also, as Fabian stated in his description of the crime scene, a caravan was parked in a nearby field. Allan Valender's barn was a mere 300 yards from where Walton died. There was also a house no more than 300 yards from the crime scene. It seems unlikely thirteen people dressed in ceremonial robes dipped in blood could dance, in the glaring light of midday, around the body of a man pinned by pitchfork to the ground and not be noticed by at least one person. Even if they did manage to pull it off, crime scene photographs show Walton's body lying very close to the hedge he was trimming, leaving little room for costumed members of a frenzied cult to dance circles around him. Surely, the villagers would have noticed if a large group of strangers were in the area the day Walton died.

The woman claimed to have been a member of the cult for some time and knew its inner-workings. She described one gathering in particular:

> People came from all over the country to attend. Animals were killed and their blood poured into goblets. The 'priests' prayed to the Devil for help. The cult believes that you get excitement and happiness from worshipping and practicing evil. The altar is a parody of a Christian altar. The Cross is placed upside down in a glass of water and the candles on a slant, almost upside down. Newcomers are initiated by being forced to drink the blood of animals. Then they all drink spirits and dance round the altar … Then they have to sign a pact in blood, giving their souls to the Devil.

Supposedly, when the woman found out about the Walton killing, she defected from the cult – but at great personal risk. As she told the *Mirror* reporter:

> Within a few days the circle of silence was put on my doorstep. It was made of twigs and graveyard chippings. It meant 'Keep Quiet'. But I could not live with myself. I told one of the leaders that I would go to the police. That night, on my way home, I was grabbed and scalped. They took a complete circle of skin and hair from my head using a doctor's scalpel.

It seems amazing that this woman, having decided to leave the clutches of a homicidal cult – one whose members think nothing of slashing an old man to death and plunging a pitchfork through him

– threatens to go to the police and is not herself murdered. It's even more amazing the cult did nothing to silence her after she went to several newspapers to publicise her ordeal. The woman was either an attention-seeker or the victim of mental illness. But who was she? In all probability, she was Sarah Jackson, a Birmingham resident who claimed to have recently severed ties with a black magic cult. She had told her story to the *Sunday Pictorial* in two articles in June 1955. In one article, she provided details of a black mass very similar to those that ran in the *Daily Mirror* story:

> There were about fifty people present. There was a small altar ... A young cockerel was killed and the blood poured into a glass to be given to those to be initiated.
> The candles were on a slant, almost upside-down, burning. A cross was placed upside down in a tumbler containing water ... The first initiate drank the blood of the sacrificed chicken, and was informed she had drunk the blood of the devil. Twisted prayers were said. She signed a pact bearing blood giving her soul to the devil in return for power ... I was initiated as a High Priestess, after my long training. Veiled, wearing my robes, I stood before the altar. Before me stood my instructor, his deputy, and a second High Priestess ... The ritual was a complete mockery of Christian worship.

The above incident supposedly took place in a Birmingham flat, which immediately seems to be an unlikely setting for such a ritual. Fifty people crammed into a small apartment with all the regalia and necessary accoutrement to perform their dark ritual? One can't help but wonder what the neighbours must have thought upon hearing a chicken being sacrificed. Not surprisingly, nothing ever came of Sarah Jackson's stories, and Walton's murder remained unsolved.

12

Fabian's Sunset

Fabian had by now retired. Having been promoted to detective superintendent on 1 July 1949, Fabian ended his twenty-eight year career as a police officer two weeks later and bid a bittersweet farewell to the halls of Scotland Yard – but he never turned his back on police work. It was in his blood. A man of good humour and lively demeanour, Fabian was a gifted storyteller – so perhaps it's not surprising he turned to writing and journalism. Indeed, it allowed him to write about the world he knew. 'Most people when they retire leave their jobs behind them,' he would write, 'but I now find myself as much concerned with the underworld as during the time when I was actually on the beat.' Shortly after his departure from the Yard, he sat down to write *Fabian of the Yard*, his first volume of memoirs, published in 1953. He details the murder of Charles Walton in a chapter titled *Under the Shadow of Meon Hill*. It's a fairly straightforward account, in which he mentions aspects of witchcraft but dismisses them as mere diversions. He tackled the topic of black magic and cults in his follow-up effort, *London After Dark*, and returned to the Walton case in his third and final book, *The Anatomy of Crime*. Reading the books today, it's interesting to note Fabian's changing view of the crime. By the time he published his last book, he was convinced – or so he wrote – that Walton's murder had been a sacrificial rite.

Fabian was a realist, but – like any author – he wanted to sell books. The witchcraft aspects of the Walton killing were firmly entrenched in the public consciousness when *The Anatomy of Crime* hit bookstores in 1970. Surely, he knew the supposed connection to the dark arts lent the killing a supernatural air. Perhaps he merely wanted to capitalise on it. He was, in essence, giving the people what they wanted. Fabian devotes a chapter to black magic in his last book, writing:

> At one time I was so appalled by the Satanists' depravity that I considered the idea of initiating criminal proceedings against them. When Aleister Crowley, the Black Magician, died in 1947 I went to his cremation at Brighton and I recognised leaders of known covens in Lewes, Shoreham, and London. But alas, while the police know only too well the havoc Black Magic cause to its victims, they need to tread wearily. Interference with any organisation that claims to be a religious sect is tricky ... Penetration of the deepest depths of witchcraft is achieved only by a complicated course of initiation, progressing from stage to stage. Intoxicated and hypnotised, even the most solid and hard-headed member of the force could succumb!

It's interesting Fabian should mention Crowley, that notorious figure 'regarded by many as evil incarnate', for Crowley's name has surfaced in connection with Charles Walton's murder. Born in 1875, Crowley was the son of a Plymouth Brethren preacher and raised a Christian. As a young man, however, he turned his back on the tenets of traditional religion and took a keen interest in magic and mysticism. In 1898, Crowley was introduced to – and subsequently joined – the Hermetic Order of the Golden Dawn. The Golden Dawn was a collective that believed they could invoke the presence of gods through magical rituals, achieving oneness with divine entities. Crowley's time with the Golden Dawn was short, as he believed its members were not true believers in the power of magic. He therefore set about developing his own esoteric ideas and beliefs, adopting the motto 'Do what thou wilt.' Many of Crowley's beliefs were rooted in carnality, for he believed sex played an intrinsic part in magic and rituals – something he expressed in his poetry:

Be strong, O man!
Lust, and enjoy all things of sense and rapture:
    Fear not that any God will deny thee for his.

He travelled extensively, always seeking new experiences and 'immersing himself in the occult'. He later claimed a mystical encounter in Cairo with a 'praeternatural' intelligence inspired the founding of his own religious philosophy, Thelema, 'a hotchpotch of all the established and defunct religions, cults, rites, and mythologies, couched in a wealth of Greek, Latin, Hebrew, Sanskrit, German, Chinese and Arabic doggerel'. He eventually established his own magical order, the Argenteum Astrum, dedicated to mystical enlightenment. Not surprisingly, Crowley was a man of eccentricities, who enjoyed animalistic sex and the performing of black magic rituals. His reputation for the weird and perverse spread, and eventually earned him the sobriquets 'The Beast' and 'The Wickedest Man in the World'. He took pleasure dressing in strange garb: wizard robes and cloaks, believing one such garment granted him the power of invisibility, and posed for numerous portraits in which he struck strange poses and showed off his unique wardrobe.

In 1920, he set up his own temple in an abandoned farmhouse in the northern Sicilian town of Cefalú and dubbed it the Abbey of Thelema. Crowley hoped to establish the cramped quarters – for there was nothing abbey-like about the abode – as a globally renowned school of magic. He envisioned acolytes making pilgrimages and paying tuition to take part in black magic rituals and immersing themselves in the Argenteum Astrum. His plan, however, met with tragic consequences. In January 1923, Raoul Loveday – a 23-year-old Oxford undergraduate – travelled to the abbey to study under the Beast. Loveday 'had a flair for poetry and the occult, and had become obsessed with Crowley's writings and longed to meet the man he so admired'.

Not long after arriving at the temple, Loveday's health began to deteriorate. In February, he passed away. Some accounts state the young man died of enteric fever, the result of drinking contaminated water from a nearby spring near the abbey. Others cite possible drug use – while another popular rumour suggested Loveday's demise was the result of drinking the blood of a cat sacrificed during one of Crowley's rituals. Loveday's death only enhanced Crowley's reputation as a purveyor of evil. Several months after Loveday's death, Crowley returned to London and ventured one afternoon to the Café Royal. 'All eyes were fixed on him and nobody spoke until the Beast had taken his seat,' notes one account. 'Only when he called for Brandy, and not freshly killed babies' blood, did the Café resume its normal hubbub.'

Crowley died, broke, in 1947, his body ravaged by heavy drinking and narcotic use; his reputation for debauchery and sinister hocus-pocus well-established. Thus, with all the talk of black magic, Satanic rituals, and the like swirling about the Walton murder, perhaps it's not surprising Crowley's name surfaced in connection with the Lower Quinton crime. The same Midlands woman who told the press in 1955 she knew who had murdered Charles Walton identified the guilty culprit as 'Mrs Crowley, the widow of Aleister Crowley'. Mrs Crowley, according to the informant, was living a quiet life in Cornwall. It transpired Mrs Crowley was actually Deirdre MacAlpine, Crowley's one-time lover. In April 1934, outside a courtroom in which Crowley was defending himself in a libel suit, MacApline – then only 19 – approached the Beast and asked, 'Couldn't I be the mother of your child?' Who was Crowley to turn down such an offer? Three years later, MacAlpine gave birth to Crowley's son. Crowley spent some time with MacAlpine in Cornwall and indulged his enthusiasm for drugs and sex. Supposedly, one of Crowley's associates also moved to the area and set up a cult, welcoming MacAlpine into its ranks. It was this cult Sarah Jackson supposedly joined, the same one responsible for Walton's murder. Superintendent Spooner reportedly investigated and dismissed the theory as ludicrous. Indeed, notes one account, 'The whole business appears to have been a classic example of rumours and gossip combined with the imaginings of a mentally deranged person.' There is certainly no record of such an investigation in the Scotland Yard case file.

And, once again, the case went nowhere.

✱

Fabian became something of an entertainment figure in his retirement. His many investigations inspired a BBC television show, *Fabian of the Yard*, broadcast over thirty-six episodes from 1954 to 1956. The show featured Bruce Seton in the starring role and concluded each week with the real Fabian sitting behind a desk, telling the audience how the case just dramatised turned out in real life. 'It was,' notes one Scotland Yard historian, 'a rather wasted exercise; for a man who was such an amusing raconteur, his televised appearances depicted him as a rather wooden-faced individual.' There was no dramatisation of the Lower Quinton murder. Three early episodes from the series were edited together and released as a movie in British cinemas in 1955.

He capitalised on his fame and enduring popularity by hitting the speakers' circuit. In South Africa in 1961, some two thousand people showed up at the city hall in Johannesburg to hear the redoubtable Fabian of the Yard speak. Civilian life, however, did not take the cop out of him. Indeed, he enthusiastically campaigned for tough sentences and corporal punishment. Such harsh measures, he believed, were necessary to combat lawlessness. In his final volume of memoirs, he wrote:

> I have investigated just about every kind of wrongdoing from petty fraud to murder. I have put scores of criminals inside; sent some to the scaffold, even. I have seen too much to be particularly surprised any more. My own immediate, personal reaction to a crime – any crime – is regret that it was allowed to happen. The crime situation in Britain is so unnecessarily serious.

In a piece he wrote for Manchester's *Empire News* on 11 July 1954, he argued the case for flogging violent prisoners. 'The only way to get a message of disapproval into such an obtuse skull is via the nine whipcord communications lines of the Home Office cat-o'-nine-tails through the flesh of his shoulders and nerves up to his selfish, destructive, jungle brain,' he opined, with his flare for language:

> Yes, I know this kind of talk is out of date. And I realise that prison floggings will also one day be out of date, just as prisons will be. I shall be glad to see that day when in some distant tomorrow we understand criminals well enough to cure them. But right now we have not reached such a stage. We still have prisons and in them we keep dangerous men. While these men exist the 'cat' must stay. And it must be used. It is the only protection prison officers have.

Fabian continued to speak, addressing Rotary Clubs and other social functions well into his later years. He still proved a popular draw, though his health was now beginning to fail. Fabian died at the age of 77 in Epsom Hospital on 14 June 1978. His death made national headlines and marked the closing of a colourful chapter in criminal history. Fabian, notes Scotland Yard historian and former police officer Dick Kirby:

> was a detective through and through. He knew his job inside and out, could run informants, knew how to squeeze the crumbs out of every bit of information and would never give up while lines of enquiry existed. Most of all, he knew how to talk to people and was able to inspire confidence in others to come and tell him what they knew. Fabian was a master murder investigator and young detectives wanted to be just like him; I know I did.

Fabian was no doubt a master of his trade with a long string of successful investigations to his name. It is then ironic that of all the cases he worked, the one that continues to intrigue is his most notable failure.

POSTSCRIPT

The clouds hung low and a light rain fell on a recent visit to Lower Quinton. Seeking shelter from the cold, I ducked into the College Arms and ordered a pint. The inside is just as a country pub should be with low-beamed ceilings and a large, stone fireplace. On this December afternoon, the fire was lit, so I took a table near the hearth and ordered the Sunday roast for lunch. As a Briton who currently lives in California, I don't often get a chance to enjoy a proper pub lunch. It was a treat. The walls of the pub are adorned with shelves cluttered with books and pictures. But there is nothing in the College Arms to inform visitors of the infamous crime that took place nearby. I didn't broach the subject with the lady who poured my beer and took my order. What would have been the point? It's no secret the residents of Lower Quinton don't like discussing the crime – and since six decades have passed since events transpired, there are likely few in the village who have any firsthand knowledge of the crime.

Nevertheless, as I ate, I imagined Alfred Potter leaning against the bar and Fabian entering the premises to ask questions. The whole thing seemed worthy of an Agatha Christie novel. Of course, in Christie's stories, the murderer always comes to light. That one of Lower Quinton's grimmest secrets is the identity of a vicious killer does not fit well with the village's bucolic setting. I pondered this – along with whether or not to order a third pint – as I ate my lunch. When done, I left to view sites associated with the crime. The rain had by now stopped, but a bitter wind blew and the sky remained overcast. The weather seemed appropriate for the purpose of my visit. From the pub, I walked the short distance to what was once Charles Walton's home. It's a beautiful cottage and had a 'For Sale' sign out front. Its appearance – at least from the outside – has changed little since that fateful morning when Walton left his house for the last time.

My gaze drifted across the lane to the gate leading into the church-yard – the gate Walton's niece, Edith, watched him walk through on his way to the fields. In an attempt to follow Walton's footsteps, I crossed the lane and entered the well-kept churchyard, with its neatly organised tombstones and colourful assortment of flowers left on various graves. I snapped a few pictures of the church and graveyard before making my way to a gate that led into the fields beyond – the gate Walton passed through the day he died. The field Walton was working in at the time of his murder is now private prop-erty – and although I felt compelled to trespass and snap a picture, I exercised restraint. Instead, all I managed was a picture of a crop of trees which concealed the murder spot from view. There was, on that day, a heaviness about the place – a sense of atmosphere that often attaches itself to a place of violent crime. No doubt the low clouds and cold wind played a part in setting the mood. Previously, I had visited Lower Quinton on a summer's afternoon and found the village utterly charming. What struck me on both visits, however, was how few people I saw walking about. It lends the place a ghostly quality. As I snapped pictures in the church yard, one person walk-ing on the opposite side of the street – the one pedestrian I saw that afternoon – cast a glance my way and carried on.

Potter died in 1974 and joined Charles Walton in eternal rest in the graveyard at St Swithin's. I surveyed several tombstones, not really believing I'd find their graves. Discussing the case with a few locals in a pub outside the town of Evesham one evening, someone told me the gravestones of both men had been removed to deter the curious from descending on the village. Potter's family remains in the area and runs the excellent Lygon Arms in Chipping Campden, an estab-lishment worthy of a visit if you're in the area.

Mindful of the graveyard's sanctity, I did not stay long, opting instead to have another stroll around the village. Again, my mind wandered back in time as I walked past some of the very doors Fabian knocked on in the course of his investigation. The Yard men – as evident by the case files – did not meet a wall of silence, as Fabian alleges in his memoirs. One can surely speculate there must have been a villager here or there who, regarding the men from the city with suspicion, kept silent – but there was certainly no outward conspiracy to thwart Fabian. On the other hand, no one seemed to volunteer any information beyond the questions posed by detectives. Was there an underlying antipathy towards Scotland Yard and its efforts to crack the case? If so, why?

As we have seen, rumours of witchcraft have persisted despite the hard facts. All one has to do is consult the Scotland Yard files to see there were no crosses carved in flesh, no willow tree overhanging the bloody scene, and no druidical stone circles nearby. Walton did not keep natterjack toads – nor is there any suggestion he attempted to converse with animals. Yet Fabian, as he put in his official report, believed the residents of Lower Quinton harboured some secret – perhaps a fearful knowledge born of local legend. If this is indeed true, it's still surprising that someone sympathetic to old Charles Walton – or his grieving niece, Edith – didn't point Fabian and Webb in the right direction. In a village of less than 500 people, it's hard to believe the killer's identity could remain a secret indefinitely.

One reason the spectre of witchcraft has so persistently shadowed the case is in no small part due to Fabian playing the angle up in his memoirs. In his final book, he dismisses witchcraft as a load of bunk – but warns readers to stay away from cults and asserts the Walton murder was a ritualistic killing. This raises a question: did Fabian, believing the murder had something to do with witchcraft, avoid mentioning the subject in his official case reports so as to escape ridicule, or did he simply decide when writing his books to give the public what they wanted? My guess is that it's the latter. It seems odd that Walton would be sacrificed in the name of some dark power and then have his clothes rummaged through.

We know from statements taken by police that some in the village believed Walton had money stashed away somewhere. We also know, by his own admission, that Potter sometimes cooked the books of his family's business to pocket extra cash. Although Fabian sought information from the War Agriculture Committee on complaints filed against Potter for shortchanging employees on their wages, the Scotland Yard case files contain no record of a response. Either Potter had some sort of money problem, or he simply liked to steal. I believe Potter killed Walton for one of two reasons:

1. He believed the old man carried around a considerable amount of money and wanted to get his hands on it.

2. He had stolen one too many times from Walton, who was now threatening to take some sort of action against his employer.

Potter's behaviour during the course of the investigation does not seem to be that of an innocent man. Why would someone, fearful they might be a homicide suspect, not immediately tell investigators they had touched one of the murder weapons? Potter can be excused for not telling Fabian he visited the murder site the day after the crime, for he did speak to a police officer. But failing to mention he disturbed the crime scene is, at the very least, suspicious. Potter also behaved strangely when Police Constable Michael Lomasney paid his first visit to The Firs after the murder. Was Potter so overcome with grief for the loss of an employee, or so ridden with guilt he couldn't look Lomasney in the face? Potter's wife said he was having trouble sleeping at night, supposedly due to what others in the village might have been thinking. Would that truly cause such emotional havoc with an innocent man? Perhaps Potter was truly saddened by Walton's unfortunate end – but his behaviour seems to hint at something more.

Of course, the most damning strikes against Potter are the various discrepancies in his statements to police. Why couldn't he keep his story straight? Perhaps he couldn't keep track of his own lies. Why Fabian never confronted Potter over the numerous inconsistencies remains a mystery – but Fabian went to his grave believing Potter to be the killer. Although Fabian was unable to bring Potter to justice, I think the circumstantial evidence confirms Fabian's suspicions.

※

There is a strange – but apocryphal – postscript to the Walton case. In August 1960, workmen were hired to remove a row of outhouses behind the cottage where Walton once lived. One workman, clearing away the dirt and debris, saw the sun reflect off something partially buried in the ground. He bent down to brush away the dirt and saw the object was an old pocket watch. Supposedly, it was identified as the watch missing from Walton's body. Opening the watchcase revealed a small piece of coloured glass. According to one account, 'the general consensus of opinion amongst the villagers was that this was a piece of witch glass, used to either reflect or absorb any evil thoughts that had been directed at its owner'.

The missing watch had been a major point of interest for the police during the Walton investigation. One would think the discovery of this vital item would have found its way into the official case files. The story cannot be authenticated – but if it's true, why did the killer return to hide the watch on his victim's property? It's yet another bizarre piece of a very bizarre puzzle. And so, the mystery remains, impervious to the theories and speculations of journalists and amateur sleuths.

In the end, only two people really know for sure what transpired in that field long ago on Valentine's Day – and like Charles Walton's lost and unmarked grave, the truth will stay forever buried.

BIBLIOGRAPHY

The Scotland Yard case files, comprised of all witness statements and Fabian's two case reports, are the primary source of information for *The Case That Foiled Fabian*. The files are catalogued at the British National Archives under catalogue number MEPO 3/2290. A number of secondary sources, however, were consulted in the writing of this book.

Details of Fabian's other adventures on the force, including his early years and training, his investigation into the IRA terror campaign of 1939, the 'Mad Emile' murder, the Robert Delaney case, the Antiquis murder, the Dagmar Peters homicide, and others are derived from his memoirs *Fabian of the Yard, London After Dark and The Anatomy of Crime*. Details on the 'Black Butterfly' murder are taken from the official case files at the British National Archives under catalogue number MEPO 3/1740.

Sources quoted and referenced in this volume are:

Books
Beynon, Mark. *London's Curse: Murder, Black Magic and Tutankhamun in the 1920s West End*. The History Press Ltd., 2011.
Conway, D.J. *Animal Magick: The Art of Recognising & Working with Familiars*. Llewellyn Publications, 1995.
Crowley, Aleister. *Magick: Book Four – Liber Aba*. Red Wheel/Weiser, LLC, 1994.
Curran, Bob. *Mysterious Celtic Mythology in American Folklore*. Pelican Publishing Company, 2010.
Dutt, W.A. *The Norfolk and Suffolk Coast*. T. Fisher Unwin, 1909.
Fabian, Robert. *Fabian of the Yard*. British Book Centre, 1953.
　London After Dark. Harlequin Books, 1954.
　The Anatomy of Crime. Pelham Books Ltd., 1970.

Grimassi, Raven. *The Witches Craft: The Roots of Witchcraft & Magical Transformation*. Llewellyn Publications, 2002.

Guiley, Rosemary. *The Encyclopedia of Witches, Witchcraft, and Wicca*. Facts on File, Inc., 1989.

Holland, Clive. *Warwickshire: The Land of Shakespeare*. Adam and Charles Black, London, 1906.

Howard, Michael. *Modern Wicca: A History from Gerald Gardner to the Present*. Llewellyn Publications, 2009.

Kirby, Dick. *The Governors: Ten of Scotland Yard's Greatest Detectives*. Wharncliffe True Crime, 2010.

Masters, Anthony. *Devil's Dominion: The Complete Story of Hell and Satanism in the Modern World*. Castle Books, 1978. McCormick, Donald. *Murder by Witchcraft: A Study of the Lower Quinton and Hagley Wood Murders*. Long, 1968.

Medway, Gareth. *The Lure of the Sinister: The Unnatural History of Satanism*. New York University Press, 2001.

Newman, Paul. *Under the Shadow of Meon Hill: The Lower Quinton and Hagley Wood Murders*. Abraxas & DGR Books, 2009.

Odell, Robin. *The Mammoth Book of Bizarre Crimes*. Constable & Robinson, 2010.

Parker, John. *At the Heart of Darkness: Witchcraft, Black Magic, and Satanism Today*. Citadel Press, 1993.

Summers, Montague. *Witchcraft and Black Magic*. Rider & Co., Ltd., 1946.

Summerscale, Kate. *The Suspicions of Mr. Whicher: A Shocking Murder and the Undoing of a Great Victorian Detective*. Walker & Company, New York, 2008.

Thomas, Donald. *An Underworld At War: Spivs, Deserters, Racketeers and Civilians in the Second World War*. John Murray, 2003.

Thrupp, John. *The Anglo-Saxon Home: A History of the Domestic Institutions and Customs of England, from the Fifth to Eleventh Century*. Longman, Green, Longman, & Roberts, London, 1862.

Wilson, Colin. *The Occult: A History*. Vintage, 1973.
Murder in the 1940s. Carroll & Graf Publishers Inc., 1993.

Periodicals

Fleming, Abraham. 'A Strange and Terrible Wonder.' Originally published in 1577. Reprinted in 1820 by J. Compton.

Morley, George. 'The Superstitions of Shakespeare's Greenwood.' *The Living Age*. Sixth Series, Volume XVI. The Living Age Company, Boston, 1897.

Simpson, Jacqueline. 'Margaret Murray: Who Believed Her, and Why?' (*Folklore* 105 (1994): 89–96.)

'Black Butterfly Is Slashed To Death In London.' *The Evening Independent*, 13 February 1939.

'Death Of Girl Gives Clue To Terrorist Ring.' *(Sarasota) Herald-Tribune*, 13 February 1939.

'More Bombs – Explosions in London.' *Sydney Morning Herald*, 26 June 1939.

'Blame Is Laid To Terrorists; 20 Are Hurt.' *The Milwaukee Journal*. 26 June 1939.

'Old Man's Terrible Injuries.' *Stratford-upon-Avon Herald*. 16 February 1945.

'Mystery. Murder. And half a century of suspense.' *The Independent*, 18 August 1999.

'Only the Cat holds back the brutes.' (Manchester) *Empire News*, 11 July 1954.

Untitled. *Daily Mail* 13 February 1954.

Murder Casebook, vol. 5, Part 71: Ritual Killings.

Websites

BBC: Uncovering Warwickshire's Sinister Secret (http://www.bbc.co.uk/coventry/features/weird-warwickshire/1945-witchcraft-murder.shtml). Referenced in chapter source notes as 'Sinister'.

English Heritage: North Gloucestershire Cotswolds NMP – World War 2 (http://www.english-heritage.org.uk/professional/research/landscapes-and-areas/national-mapping-programme/north-gloucestershire-cotswolds-nmp/north-gloc-cotswolds-nmp-ww2/). Referenced in chapter source notes as 'Heritage'.

Rollright Stones (http://www.rollrightstones.co.uk) Referenced in chapter source notes as 'Rollright'.

The Red Horse of Tysoe. (http://www.hows.org.uk/personal/hillfigs/lost/tysoe/tysoe.htm). Referenced in chapter source notes as 'Red Horse'.

Witchcraft Murder in Long Compton. (http://www.rootsweb.ancestry.com/~engcbanb/families/jeavons/jeavons01.htm). Referenced in the chapter source notes as 'Jeavons'.

Occultebooks: So how old is Witchcraft really? (http://www.occultebooks.com/articles/de_theroleofMargaretMurray.htm). Referenced in chapter source notes as 'Occulte'.

England: The Other Within: Margaret Murray. (http://england.prm.ox.ac.uk/englishness-Margaret-Murray.html). Referenced in chapter source notes as 'England'.

Strange but True: Mysterious and Bizarre People (excerpt – Barnes and Noble Books, New York, 1998) by Thomas Slemen. (http://thomasslemen.tripod.com/walton.html). Referenced in chapter source notes as 'Slemen'.

Charles Walton – 50 Years On. (http://www.whitedragon.org.uk/articles/ charles.htm). Referenced in chapter source notes as 'White Dragon'.

Warwickshire Life: Long Compton's Bewitched Past (http://www. warwickshirelife.co.uk/people/long_compton_s_bewitched_past_ warwickshire_life_1_1632149). Referenced in chapter source notes as 'Warwickshire'.

Wormwood Chronicles: The Premiere eZine for the Underground Scene. (https://sites.google.com/a/wormwoodchronicles.com/wormwood- chronicles/wormwoodfiles/charles-walton-murder). Referenced in chapter source notes as 'Wormwood'.

NOTES

Unless otherwise noted, information is derived from the official case files.

Chapter 1: Origins of a Mystery

1. Details on the various legends surrounding the creation of Meon Hill. Sinister.
2. 'king was lord of departed spirits ...' Sinister.
3. 'as famous as any figure ...' *Murder Casebook*, vol. 71, p. 2,573.
4. 'found lying face-up beneath a willow tree on Meon Hill ...' Guiley, p. 361.
5. 'was found after a day's work ...' Masters, p. 159.
6. Wilson's referencing of a willow tree. *The Occult*. Wilson, p. 419.
7. Parker's referencing of a willow tree. Parker, p. 38.
8. 'The Willow tree (*Salix alba*) is associated ...' Grimassi, p. 193.
9. 'As the Anglo-Saxons were very reckless ...' Thrupp, p. 271.
10. 'The crops of 1944 had been poor ...' Guiley, p. 361.
11. 'Walton had been pinned to the ground ...' *Murder Casebook*, vol. 71, p. 2,524.
12. 'The body of the old man was badly mutilated ...' Curran, p. 117.
13. 'A cross-shaped wound had been slashed ...' Guiley, p. 361.
14. 'injuries were hideous ...' *Yard*. Fabian, p. 105.
15. 'stern-eyed cops striding from house to house ...' Newman, pp. 57–58.

Chapter 2: A Detective's Education

16. 'about as well as a recluse at a holiday camp ...' *Yard*. Fabian, p. 14.
17. 'Like most youngsters of my generation ...' *Yard*. Fabian, p. 14.
18. 'I remember what struck me most ...' *Yard*. Fabian, p. 14.
19. '5 feet 10 inches, tall enough ...' *Yard*. Fabian, p. 14.
20. 'British birth and pure British descent.' *Yard*. Fabian, p. 14.
21. 'On the beat an officer should normally walk ...' *Yard*. Fabian, p. 15.
22. 'Walking the streets of the West End ...' *Dark*. Fabian, p. 11.
23. 'eight feet by seven feet ...' *Yard*. Fabian, p. 17.
24. 'It was a good life in most ways ...' *Yard*. Fabian, p. 17.
25. 'This might save you time.' Based on a paraphrased statement in *Yard*. Fabian, p. 19.
26. 'opposite side of the road ...' *Yard*. Fabian, p. 19.
27. 'clubs, brothels, betting houses ...' *Dark*. Fabian, p. 10.
28. 'very independent.' *Yard*. Fabian, p. 16.
29. 'Battling Annie' *Yard*. Fabian, p. 16.
30. 'I soon realised that if I was to beat the crook ...' *Yard*. Fabian, p. 18.
31. 'first appearance on the street ...' *Yard*. Fabian, p. 17.
32. 'ghost.' *Yard*. Fabian, p. 22.
33. 'I doubt if any young man in London ...' *Yard*. Fabian, p. 22.
34. 'The Little Water Drinker.' *Yard*. Fabian, p. 23.
35. 'I found it following me ...' *Yard*. Fabian, p. 23.
36. 'You all right ... All right.' *Dark*. Fabian, p. 19.
37. 'Well done, Robert.' *Dark*. Fabian, p. 20.
38. 'of little value without previous practical experience ...' *Yard*. Fabian, p. 20.
39. 'quick, agile as a cat.' *Yard*. Fabian, p. 34.
40. 'the porous tread of crepe shoes.' *Yard*. Fabian, p. 37.
41. 'R. Radd, 52, Half Moon-street ...' *Yard*. Fabian, p. 37.
42. 'Those were the days of evening clothes ...' *Yard*. Fabian, p. 38.
43. 'the dossier of almost every crook in Europe ...' *Yard*. Fabian, p. 161.
44. 'I suppose it's too much to hope ...' *Yard*. Fabian, p. 39.
45. 'could apparently climb the sheer side of a house.' *Yard*. Fabian, p. 33.

Chapter 3: Fabian Arrives

46. 'the other was lost ...' Summerscale, p. 68.
47. 'The County Police, excluding a few large provincial cities ...' Tullet, p. 9.
48. 'be specially designated for Home Office service ...' Tullet, p. 10.
49. 'two weeks on the drill square ...' Tullet, p. 13.
50. 'a notoriously violent gang.' *Yard*. Fabian, p. 106.

51. 'Telephone the C.I.D. commander.' *Yard*. Fabian, p. 106.
52. 'check the torches in one of the murder bags.' *Yard*. Fabian, p. 106.
53. 'There are nine brown leather murder bags ...' *Yard*. Fabian, p. 106.
54. 'heart and other internal organs.' Tullet, p. 66.
55. 'What motive ... the work of a maniac.' *Yard*. Fabian, p. 106.
56. 'On the hilltops around Lower Quinton ...' *Yard*. Fabian, p. 105.
57. 'because of the conspiratorial way ...' Rollright.
58. King Stone's original purpose a mystery. Rollright.
59. 'with ambitions to conquer all of England.' Rollright.
60. 'Seven long strides ... and I myself an elder tree.' Rollright.
61. 'if cut when in blossom will bleed.' Rollright.
62. 'steal out to the mysterious Rollright Stones ...' Guiley, p. 361.
63. 'the 493 villagers of Lower Quinton ...' *Yard*. Fabian, p. 109.
64. 'with map pins, little coloured flags and threads.' *Yard*. Fabian, p. 109.
65. 'then show where the paths crossed ...' *Yard*. Fabian, p. 109.
66. 'We had brought the 20th Century ...' *Yard*. Fabian, p. 109.
67. 'showed even the bloodstains ...' *Yard*. Fabian, p. 109.
68. 'Old Man's Terrible Injuries.' *Stratford-on-Avon Herald*, 16 February 1945.

Chapter 4: Fabian of the Yard

69. 'They were bad characters ...' *Yard*. Fabian, p. 23.
70. 'sir.' *Yard*. Fabian, p. 23.
71. 'What happened ...?' *Yard*. Fabian, p. 24.
72. 'Yes, policeman ...' *Yard*. Fabian, p. 24.
73. 'He was an acrobat.' *Yard*. Fabian, p. 24.
74. 'prickly as a hairbrush.' *Yard*, Fabian, p. 22.
75. 'In an instant ...' *Yard*. Fabian, p. 25.
76. 'under scarlet lampshades.' *Yard*. Fabian, p. 26.
77. 'What about overtime ... Scotland Yard.' *Yard*. Fabian, p. 26.
78. 'In answering the ever-ringing telephones ...' Kirby, p. 89.
79. 'detective sergeant (second class).' Kirby, p. 89.
80. 'in broad daylight and walk away ...' *Yard*. Fabian, p. 153.
81. 'gutter musicians, beggars ...' *Yard*. Fabian, p. 154.
82. 'Like most jobs ...' *Yard*. Fabian, p. 20.
83. Unless otherwise noted, all details and quoted material pertaining to 'The Black Butterfly' case comes from the official case file, catalogued under MEPO 3/1740 at the British National Archives.
84. 'she was a fluttering, black-haired beauty.' *The Evening Independent*, 13 February 1939.
85. 'The Black Butterfly's ornaments, small toys ...' *Yard*. Fabian, p. 160.
86. 'The stiletto slaying of a comely Irish girl ...' *The Herald Tribune*,

13 February 1939.

87. Unless otherwise noted, all details and quoted material from Fabian's investigation into the IRA ring targeting London is derived from his memoir *Fabian of the Yard*, pp. 64–68.

88. 'that two men drove up in a taxi ...' *Sydney Morning Herald*, 26 June 1939.

89. Man rescued by angry crowd. *The Milwaukee Journal*, 26 June 1939.

90. 'no Scotland Yard officer ...' Thomas, p. 9.

Chapter 5: The Suspect

All information in this chapter is derived from the official case files.

Chapter 6: An Unyielding Puzzle

91. 'training and transit camps used by thousands of troops.' Heritage.

92. 'office table and workbench.' *Dark*. Fabian, p. 9.

93. 'consists of knowing everybody and winning their friendship ...' *Dark*. Fabian, p. 9.

94. Fabian's favourite pubs. *Dark*. Fabian, pp. 78–79.

Chapter 7: Suspicions Abound

All information in this chapter is derived from the official case files.

Chapter 8: Beyond the Case Files

95. 'The practice of Black Magic ...' *Dark*. Fabian, p. 72.

96. 'posed a menace to society.' *Crime*. Fabian, p. 184.

97. 'obsessed with witchcraft and abnormal violence.' *Crime*. Fabian, p. 185.

98. 'Witchcraft can break up marriages ...' *Crime*. Fabian, pp. 184–185.

99. 'occult magic circles.' Medway, p. 353.

100. 'the celebration of masses, magical litanies ...' Summers, p. 180.

101. '"Inquisitors" dressed in monks' cowls ...' *Dark*. Fabian, p. 75.

102. 'They do not realise ...' *Dark*. Fabian, p. 73.

103. 'the girl had been hypnotised ...' *Dark*. Fabian, p. 73.

104. 'The student, if he attains any success ...' Crowley, p. 613.

105. 'a house converted into flatlest.' *Crime*. Fabian, p. 187.

106. 'This is the entrance ...' *Crime*. Fabian, p. 187.

107. 'obscenely fashioned' ... 'with chants and responses intoned in Latin.' *Crime*. Fabian, p. 187.

108. 'When the communion wafers ...' *Crime*. Fabian, p. 187.
109. 'excited terror and brought out the worst in people.' *Crime*. Fabian, p. 187.
110. 'This is the more remarkable bearing ...' Morley, p. 60.
111. 'One magpie means sorrow ...' Morley, p. 61.
112. 'successive generations of landowners and visitors.' Red Horse.
113. 'All the little, lonely villages ...' Morley, p. 62.
114. 'will not pass from Bidford ...' *Yard*. Fabian, p. 105.
115. 'night coach' ... 'peculiar in woody districts.' Morley, p. 62.
116. 'Among the villages of the plain ...' quoted in Gardner, p. 233.
117. 'with a short tail, the face of an ape.' Guiley, p. 24.
118. 'Shuck' ... 'graveyards, lonely country roads ...' Guiley, p. 24.
119. 'The church did as it were quake and stagger ...' Dutt, p. 85.
120. 'moved such admiration ...' Dutt, p. 85.
121. 'The Black Dog, the Devil in such a likeness ...' Dutt, p. 85.
122. 'as shrunken as a piece of leather ...' Fleming, p. 12.
123. 'being partaker of the people's perplexity.' Fleming, p. 13.
124. 'a wonderful example of God's wrath ...' Fleming, p. 11.
125. 'As testimonies and witnesses ...' Fleming, p. 13.
126. 'For the remainder of his 74 years ...' Guiley, p. 361.
127. 'slaughterhouse horror.' *Crime*. Fabian, p. 190.
128. 'a retriever.' *Crime*. Fabian, p. 190.
129. 'Looking for your dog?' ... 'A black dog.' *Crime*. Fabian, p. 190.
130. 'The Ghost.' *Crime*. Fabian, p. 190.
131. 'realised for certain we were up against witchcraft.' *Crime*. Fabian, p. 190.
132. 'We made our investigation in the village ...' *Yard*. Fabian, p. 110.
133. 'When Albert Webb and I walked into the village pub ...' *Yard*. Fabian, p. 110.
134. 'I'm inquiring about the late Charles Walton' ... '... What are you worrying about?' *Yard*. Fabian, p. 110.

Chapter 9: The Spectre of Witchcraft

135. 'Anybody can become a witch ...' *Yard*. Fabian, p. 105.
136. 'In the village some interesting and ancient customs ...' Holland, pp. 303–304.
137. 'Willful murder, deliberately stabbed to death ...' Jeavons.
138. 'A terrible aspect of the entire affair.' *Crime*. Fabian, p. 191.
139. 'There is no evidence whatsoever ...' Quoted in Newman, p. 96.
140. Unless otherwise noted below, all details on the Hagley Wood murder are derived from *Murder Casebook*, pp. 2,536—2,541.
141. 'Trees are magickal beings ...' Grimassi, p. 171.

142. 'a middle-aged and highly-respected...' Occulte.
143. 'witches were members ...' England.
144. 'The very act of placing a body ...' Quoted in Newman, p. 82.
145. The details of Anna, the Dutchman, British officer, and trapeze artist. *The Independent.* 18 August 1999.
146. 'both MI5 and the police ...' *The Independent.* 18 August 1999.

Chapter 10: No End in Sight

147. 'Edith confirmed her uncle ...' *Murder Casebook*, p. 2,531.
148. 'I have never said this publicly before ...' *Crime.* Fabian, p. 191.
149. Unless otherwise noted, all details and quoted information on the Dagmar Peters murder is taken from *Fabian of the Yard*, pp. 136–140.
150. 'the bag had been thrown into a stream ...' Odell, p. 284.
151. 'I have no doubts ...' *Yard.* Fabian, p. 21.
152. Details and quoted information on the Antiquis murder is taken from *Fabian of the Yard*, pp. 80–93.
153. 'a fitting end to a tremendous career.' Kirby, p. 100.

Chapter 11: The Mystery's Allure

154. 'It is almost certain ...' quoted in Newman, p. 54.
155. 'Walton had quite a sinister reputation ...' Slemen.
156. 'Walton had been seen on many occasions ...' Slemen.
157. 'was widely known to have clairvoyant powers ...' Guiley, p. 361.
158. Wilson makes his assertion in his book *The Occult*, p. 420.
159. 'demonic toads.' *Wormwood.*
160. 'as creatures of the devil.' Conway, p. 213.
161. 'I think there are still remnants ...' McCormick, p. 68.
162. 'He wouldn't kill them ...' quoted in Newman, p. 97.
163. 'to interfere with or destroy ...' Guiley, p. 25.
164. 'killing could hardly have been more public ...' *Warwickshire.*
165. 'Ask in these parts ...' *Daily Mirror*, 13 February 1954.
166. 'Now, here are some of the coincidences ... I am pledged not to reveal it.' *Daily Mirror*, 13 February 1954.
167. 'The lack of motive was puzzling ...' Gardner, p. 231.
168. 'relate to the Sun, the Moon, and the Zodiac ...' Gardner, p. 231.
169. Nothing to do with black magic rituals. Gardner, p. 231.
170. 'Shortly after we started ...' McCormick, p. 115.
171. A shadow descends on Mr Mills' home. Newman, pp. 63–64.
172. 'I let myself be seen ...' *Murder Casebook*, p. 2,555.
173. 'A terrified woman ...' quoted in Medway, p. 150.

174. 'A woman has come forward ...' quoted in Medway, p. 150.
175. 'Thirteen people took part in the ceremony ...' quoted in Medway, p. 151.
176. 'People came from all over the country to attend ...' quoted in Medway, p. 151.
177. 'Within a few days the circle of silence ...' quoted in Gardner, p. 221.
178. 'There were about fifty people present ...' quoted in Gardner, pp. 201–202.
179. What the neighbours might have thought. Gardner, p. 202.

Chapter 12: Fabian's Sunset

180. Fabian's promotion and retirement. Kirby, p. 100.
181. 'Most people when they retire ...' *Dark*. Fabian, p. 3.
182. 'At one time I was so appalled ...' *Crime*. Fabian, p. 188.
183. 'regarded by many as evil incarnate.' *Murder Casebook*, p. 2,534.
184. 'Be strong, O man! ...' *Murder Casebook*, p. 2,535.
185. 'immersing himself in the occult.' Beynon, p. 104.
186. 'praeternatural.' Beynon, p. 105.
187. 'a hotchpotch of all the established ...' Beynon, p. 105.
188. 'had a flair for poetry ...' Beynon, p. 119.
189. 'All eyes were fixed on him ...' quoted in Beynon, p. 128.
190. 'Mrs Crowley, the widower of Aleister Crowley.' Howard p. 141.
191. 'Couldn't I be the mother of your child?' quoted in Beynon, p. 158.
192. Crowley in Cornwall. Howard, p. 142.
193. 'The whole business appears to have been ...' Howard, p. 142.
194. 'It was a rather wasted exercise ...' Kirby, p. 100.
195. 'I have investigated ...' *Crime*. Fabian, pp. 13–14.
196. 'The only way to get message of disapproval ...' *Empire News*, 11 July 1954.
197. 'was a detective through and through ...' Kirby, pp. 103–104.

Postscript

198. 'the general consensus of opinion ...' White Dragon.

INDEX

Lightning Source UK Ltd.
Milton Keynes UK
UKOW04f1944160514

231811UK00001B/1/P